W9-BKA-795

Better Homes and Gardens®
NEW
JUNIOR
COOK BOOK

BETTER HOMES AND GARDENS
TEST KITCHEN®

Our seal assures you that every recipe in the *New Junior Cook Book*
has been tested in the Better Homes and Gardens® Test Kitchen.
This means that each recipe is practical and reliable,
and meets our high standards of taste appeal.

BETTER HOMES AND GARDENS® BOOKS

Editor: Gerald M. Knox
Art Director: Ernest Shelton
Managing Editor: David A. Kirchner
Editorial Project Managers: Liz Anderson, James D. Blume,
  Marsha Jahns, Jennifer Speer Ramundt, Angela K. Renkoski

Department Head, Cook Books: Sharyl Heiken
Associate Department Heads: Sandra Granseth,
  Rosemary C. Hutchinson, Elizabeth Woolever
Senior Food Editors: Linda Henry, Marcia Stanley, Joyce Trollope
Associate Food Editors: Jennifer Darling, Heather M. Hephner,
  Mary Major, Shelli McConnell, Mary Jo Plutt
Test Kitchen: Director, Sharon Stilwell; Photo Studio Director,
  Janet Herwig; Home Economists: Lynn Blanchard, Kay Cargill,
  Marilyn Cornelius, Maryellyn Krantz, Marge Steenson,
  Colleen Weeden

Associate Art Directors: Neoma Thomas, Linda Ford Vermie,
  Randall Yontz
Assistant Art Directors: Lynda Haupert, Harijs Priekulis,
  Tom Wegner
Graphic Designers: Mary Schlueter Bendgen, Michael Burns,
  Brenda Lesch
Art Production: Director, John Berg; Associate, Joe Heuer;
  Office Manager, Michaela Lester

President, Book Group: Jeramy Lanigan
Vice President, Retail Marketing: Jamie L. Martin
Vice President, Administrative Services: Rick Rundall

BETTER HOMES AND GARDENS® MAGAZINE
President, Magazine Group: James A. Autry
Editorial Director: Doris Eby
Food and Nutrition Editor: Nancy Byal

MEREDITH CORPORATION OFFICERS
Chairman of the Executive Committee: E. T. Meredith III
Chairman of the Board: Robert A. Burnett
President: Jack D. Rehm

New Junior Cook Book

Editor: Mary Major
Editorial Project Manager: Liz Anderson
Graphic Designer: Mary Schlueter Bendgen
Electronic Text Processor: Paula Forest
Food Stylists: Lynn Blanchard, Janet Herwig
Contributing Illustrators: Thomas Rosborough, Steve Shock
Contributing Photographers: Michael Jensen (p. 37), Scott Little

On the front cover: *Just-My-Size Pizzas* (see recipe, page 23)

Contents

4 Getting Started
Hints for young cooks.

10 Breakfast Dishes
Egg dishes, pancakes, and French toast for the first meal of the day.

20 Bread Spreads
Deliciously simple bread toppers and fillings.

22 Great Snacks
Tasty treats for after-school or anytime snacking.

34 Fruit Fix-Ups
Serve as desserts, snacks, or part of the meal.

36 Sandwiches
Create super sandwiches for lunch or supper.

48 Main Dishes
Treat your parents by making one of these taste-tempting dishes for dinner.

64 Vegetable Nibbles
Dips and spreads turn vegetables into delicious snacks.

66 Desserts
An assortment of yummy cookies, scrumptious cakes, and other luscious sweets.

76 The Basic Food Groups
Some tips for smart eating to keep you healthy.

78 Nutrition Analysis Chart

80 Index

Getting Started

Cooking is fun. That's what our kid-testers told us when they made and tasted all the recipes in this book. To join in the fun, find a recipe. Carefully read it through, assemble the equipment and ingredients you'll need, and you're ready to cook.

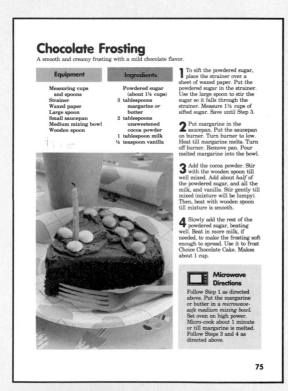

Here are some tips for reading the recipes in this book.

Equipment

Under the blue heading, you'll find the equipment list. This gives all the utensils, pans, and other items you will need. The recipes in this book use basic equipment found in most kitchens. But, if you are missing an item, ask your mom or dad for help.

Ingredients

Under the pink heading, you'll find an ingredient list. You may need to buy some ingredients. Write down the items you need on a piece of paper. Then show it to your mom or dad and ask if you can buy them.

Recipe Directions

To the right of the ingredient list, you'll find the recipe directions. They are broken down into numbered steps. Always finish one step before you start another step.

Purple Boxes

Throughout the book, you'll notice purple boxes. These are recipe variations. Some tell you how to make the recipe in the microwave oven (see tip, *page 23*). Others contain a few changes from the basic recipe and make a completely different dish.

When making a variation, be sure to read both the basic recipe and the purple box, because the purple box refers to steps in the basic recipe.

As you look through this book, you'll see some pages with a red apple. These recipes are so easy, you can make them without adult help. Just let Mom or Dad know that no sharp knives or heating are needed.

Points To Remember

As with any activity, taking certain steps in the kitchen keeps cooking safe. Here are a few tips to ensure enjoyable cooking.

Safety Tips

Always use hot pads to handle anything hot. Remember that anything you take from the oven, microwave oven, or stove will be hot and will stay hot for a while.

When cooking food on top of the stove, turn the handle of the pan or skillet to the middle of the stove. This keeps you from bumping the handle and spilling the hot food.

Be sure an adult is around when you use the oven, the stove, a sharp knife, or an electric appliance, like a mixer or a blender.

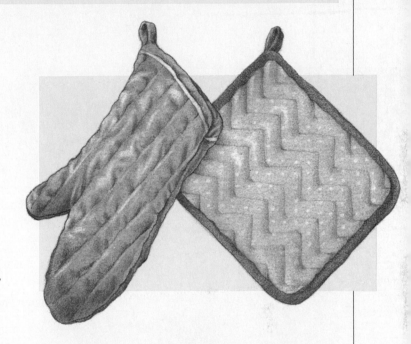

Other Hints

Before you start to cook, wash your hands with lots of soap and water. Also, it's a good idea to wear an apron to keep your clothes clean.

Keep a damp cloth or paper towel nearby to wipe up anything you spill. It makes cleanup go faster and prevents people from slipping on food spilled on the floor.

One final point: Clean up the kitchen when you're finished. Put away all the ingredients and equipment you have used. Wash and dry dishes (or put them in the dishwasher). Wipe off counters and tables. Then, your mom and dad will be happy to let you cook another time.

Measuring Up

Careful measuring makes a successful recipe. You'll need a liquid measuring cup, a set of measuring cups for dry ingredients, and a set of measuring spoons (see page 8).

Liquids

Liquid measuring cups have spouts that make pouring easy and lines that mark different measurements. Use these cups or measuring spoons to measure ingredients such as water, milk, juice, and honey.

To measure in a cup, place the measuring cup on a flat surface. Add some liquid. Then, bend down so your eyes are even with the measurement marks. If you don't have enough liquid, pour in a little more. Then, check again. Do this until you have the right amount. If you have too much liquid, pour out the extra.

To measure in a measuring spoon, hold it over a bowl and add liquid to fill the spoon.

Dry Ingredients

Use dry measuring cups or measuring spoons to measure dry ingredients like flour and sugar. Dry measuring cups usually come in sets of four. Each cup measures a different amount—1 cup, ½ cup, ⅓ cup, and ¼ cup.

Use the measuring cup or measuring spoon that is the size you need. Spoon the ingredient into the cup or spoon. Then, level it off with a narrow metal spatula. For ⅔ cup, measure ⅓ cup. Pour out the ingredient and measure another ⅓ cup. For ¾ cup, measure ½ cup and ¼ cup. Together they equal ¾ cup.

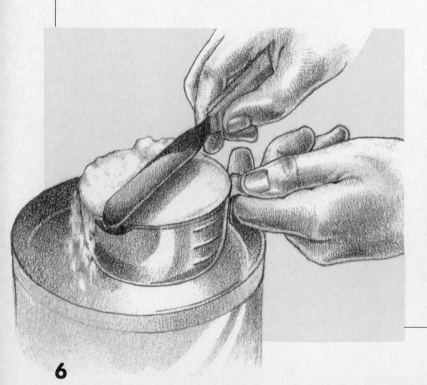

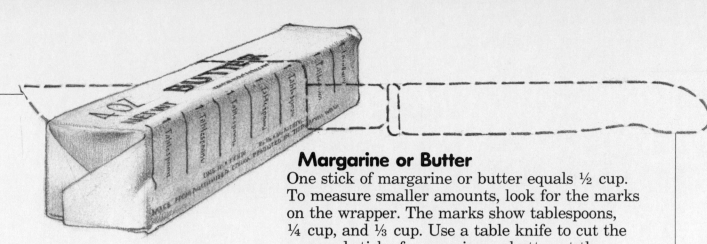

Margarine or Butter

One stick of margarine or butter equals ½ cup. To measure smaller amounts, look for the marks on the wrapper. The marks show tablespoons, ¼ cup, and ⅓ cup. Use a table knife to cut the wrapped stick of margarine or butter at the mark you need. Then unwrap it.

Shortening and Peanut Butter

Use dry measuring cups to measure shortening and peanut butter. Pack the shortening or peanut butter into the measuring cup with a rubber scraper. Cut through the shortening with the rubber scraper to squeeze out all the air. When the measuring cup is full, level off the top with the flat edge of the rubber scraper or a narrow metal spatula. To remove the shortening or peanut butter from the measuring cup, run the rubber scraper around the inside of the cup and push the ingredient out. Be sure to scrape it all out.

Brown Sugar

Brown sugar sometimes clumps, so you measure it differently than other sugars. To measure brown sugar, pack it into the dry measuring cup with your fingers. Press down. Add brown sugar till it is level with the top of the measuring cup. When you dump out the brown sugar, it should hold the shape of the cup.

Words to Cook By

When reading a recipe, you may find a word or phrase that's new to you. These pages explain some common cooking terms.

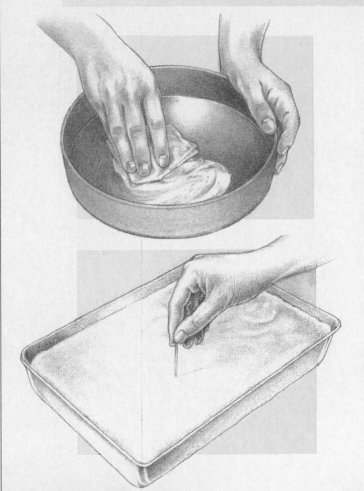

Greasing Pans

To keep cakes, muffins, and some other foods from sticking to the baking pan, you need to grease the pan. Put some shortening on a small piece of paper towel or waxed paper. Then, spread it over the inside bottom and sides of the pan.

Testing Cakes for Doneness

Test cakes after the shortest baking time given in the recipe. Stick a wooden toothpick in the center. Pull the toothpick out. If the toothpick comes out clean or has only a few crumbs sticking to it, the cake is done. If wet batter clings to the toothpick, return the cake to the oven for a few more minutes and test again. Test cupcakes or brownies the same way.

Colanders

Colanders are handy for draining liquids from foods. A colander looks like a bowl but has lots of small holes for the liquid to flow through. You can use a large strainer in place of a colander.

Teaspoons and Tablespoons

Measuring teaspoons and tablespoons differ from the ones you eat with. A set of measuring spoons includes ¼ teaspoon, ½ teaspoon, 1 teaspoon, and 1 tablespoon. One tablespoon equals 3 teaspoons.

What's a Dash?

Recipes sometimes call for a dash of an ingredient. A dash is a small amount. It's much less than ¼ teaspoon. To add a dash of an ingredient, just sprinkle a little out of the can or jar.

Cooking till Bubbly

Many times when you cook food on top of the stove, a recipe tells you to cook till bubbly. Look for lots of big bubbles that form quickly, then break. This also is called boiling.

Simmering

Foods simmer when lots of small bubbles come to the surface and break gently. To simmer food, cook over high heat till bubbly. Then, turn the burner to low. Cover the mixture with a lid, if it says to in the recipe.

Slicing and Chopping

Ask an adult for help with slicing and chopping when you need to use a sharp knife. Always slice or chop food on a cutting board. Never cut food while holding it in your hands.

To slice a food, hold the food firmly on the board. With a sharp knife, cut a thin piece off the end of the food. Repeat till all the food is cut. Try to make all the pieces about the same thickness.

When you want to chop a food, slice it first. Then, cut the slices into lots of small pieces that are about the same size. The shape of the pieces doesn't matter.

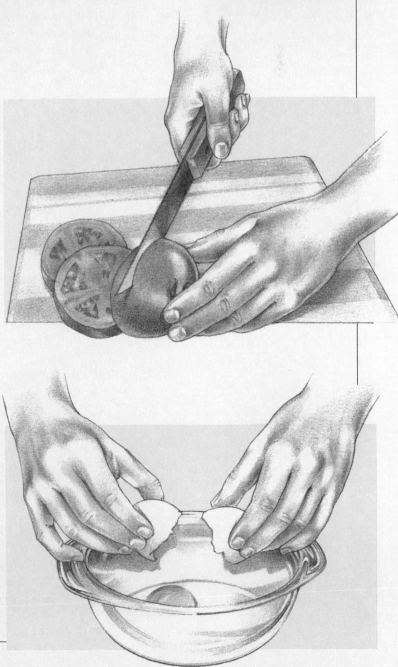

Cracking an Egg

To crack an egg, tap it with a table knife around the middle till it starts to crack. Working over a bowl, pull the eggshell halves apart and let the egg fall into the bowl. If pieces of eggshell fall into the bowl, lift them out with your fingers.

Scrambled Eggs

Put the eggs in the jar and give it a good shake to mix them up.

Equipment	Ingredients
Measuring cups and spoons Table knife Wide-mouth jar with screw-top lid (like a mayonnaise *or* peanut butter jar) Large skillet Wooden spoon	8 eggs ¼ cup milk ¼ teaspoon salt Dash pepper 1 tablespoon margarine *or* butter Cooked bacon pieces *or* shredded American cheese (if you like)

1 Crack an egg into the jar. Repeat with the remaining eggs. Add milk, salt, and pepper to the jar. Tightly screw the lid on the jar. Shake till the whites and yolks are well mixed with the other ingredients.

2 Put the margarine or butter in the skillet. Put the skillet on a burner. Turn the burner to medium heat. When the margarine bubbles, pour the egg mixture into the skillet. Cook for 1 minute. *Do not stir.*

3 After the 1 minute is over, stir the egg mixture gently with the spoon. Cook about 4 minutes, stirring often, or till eggs are firm but still moist and shiny. Turn off burner. Remove skillet. Sprinkle eggs with bacon or cheese, if you like. Serves 4.

 Microwave Directions

Follow Step 1. Put the margarine or butter in a *1-quart microwave-safe bowl*. Do not cover. Put the bowl in the microwave oven. Set on high (100%) power. Micro-cook for 30 seconds or till margarine melts. Pour egg mixture into bowl. Micro-cook for 4 minutes. After each minute, push the cooked part to center of bowl with a *rubber scraper*. If the eggs are still runny, micro-cook 10 to 60 seconds more. Serve as above.

Baked Ham Omelet

Wrap the omelet squares around the creamy ham filling.

Equipment	Ingredients
Measuring cups and spoons	2 2½-ounce packages very thinly sliced ham
Table knife	1 3-ounce package cream cheese with chives
Medium saucepan with lid	1 tablespoon milk
Wooden spoon	12 eggs
Medium mixing bowl	¼ cup water
Eggbeater *or* fork	Dash pepper
15x10x1-inch baking pan	2 tablespoons margarine *or* butter
Hot pads	
Pancake turner	
6 plates	

1 Turn the oven to 400°. For the filling, cut the ham into thin strips using the table knife. Cut the cream cheese into small pieces. In the saucepan, put the ham, cream cheese, and milk. Put the pan on a burner. Turn the burner to low heat. Cook and stir with the wooden spoon until the cream cheese is melted. Turn off the burner. Remove the saucepan from the burner. Cover with the lid. Save until Step 5.

2 Crack the eggs into the mixing bowl. Add water and pepper. Use the eggbeater or fork to beat till well mixed.

3 Place margarine or butter in the baking pan. Place the pan in the oven. Heat about 2 minutes or till margarine is melted. Using hot pads, carefully tilt the pan so the melted margarine coats the pan. Place the pan on the oven rack. Carefully pour the egg mixture into the pan.

4 Bake for 6 to 7 minutes or till the egg mixture is set but still shiny. Use hot pads to remove the pan from the oven. Cut into 6 squares.

5 Use the pancake turner to put one square on a plate. Turn the square upside-down. Then, turn the square so one corner is toward you. Spoon some of the filling on the half of the square closest to you. Fold the other half over the filling, making a triangle. Repeat with the remaining squares and filling. Makes 6 servings.

Chocolate French Toast

To make plain French toast, use regular milk in place of chocolate milk.

Equipment	Ingredients

Measuring cups
Table knife
Small mixing bowl
Eggbeater or fork
9-inch pie plate
Large skillet
Pancake turner
	2 eggs
	½ cup chocolate-
	    flavored milk
	2 tablespooons
	    margarine
	    or butter
	4 slices bread
	Sifted powdered
	    sugar (if you like)
	Canned cherry pie
	    filling *or*
	    raspberry *or*
	    strawberry
	    syrup (if you like)

1 Crack the eggs into the mixing bowl. Beat with the eggbeater or fork till the yolks and whites are mixed. Add the chocolate-flavored milk. Beat till well mixed. Pour the egg mixture into the pie plate.

2 Put *half* of the margarine or butter in the skillet. Put the skillet on a burner. Turn the burner to medium-high heat.

3 Dip one slice of the bread into the egg mixture. Turn the bread over to coat the other side. Put the coated bread in the skillet. Repeat with another slice of bread.

4 Cook till the bottoms are brown. To see if the bottoms are brown, lift the bread with the pancake turner and peek underneath. Turn the bread over with the pancake turner. Cook till the other side is brown. Remove the bread from the skillet with the pancake turner.

5 Put the remaining margarine or butter in the skillet. Repeat Steps 3 and 4 with the remaining bread and egg mixture. Turn off the burner. Remove the skillet from the burner. Sprinkle French toast with powdered sugar and top with cherry pie filling or syrup, if you like. Serves 2.

Raisin Pancake Squares

These pancakes turn out square because you make them in a baking pan.

Equipment	Ingredients
Measuring cups and spoons	Shortening
Paper towel *or* waxed paper	1 egg
15x10x1-inch baking pan	2 cups packaged pancake mix
Table knife	1½ cups milk
Medium mixing bowl	2 tablespoons cooking oil
Wooden spoon	1 teaspoon ground cinnamon
Rubber scraper	½ cup raisins *or* mixed dried fruit bits
Hot pads	Margarine *or* butter (if you like)
Pancake turner	Maple *or* maple-flavored syrup

1 Turn the oven to 425°. Put some shortening on a piece of paper towel or waxed paper. Spread the shortening over the bottom of the baking pan. Save until Step 3.

2 Crack the egg into the mixing bowl. Add the pancake mix, milk, cooking oil, and cinnamon. Stir with the wooden spoon till the dry ingredients are wet. (The batter should have small lumps, so don't stir too much.) Stir in raisins or dried fruit bits.

3 Pour the batter into the greased baking pan. Use the rubber scraper to scrape all of the batter from the mixing bowl into the pan. Spread the batter evenly in the pan.

4 Put the pan in the oven. Bake about 10 minutes or till the edges are light brown and the top springs back when you lightly touch it with your finger. Use hot pads to remove the pan from the oven. Cut into 6 squares. Then, cut each square into 4 smaller squares. Lift the squares from the pan using the pancake turner. Spread with margarine or butter, if you like. Serve with syrup. Serves 6.

Applesauce Breakfast Cake

Delicious for breakfast, snacks, or dessert.

Equipment

Measuring cups
and spoons
Paper towel *or*
waxed paper
8x8x2-inch baking
pan
Small mixing bowl
Wooden spoon
Waxed paper
Large mixing bowl
Table knife
Rubber scraper
Wooden toothpick
Hot pads
Cooling rack

Ingredients

Shortening
¼ cup packed brown
sugar
1 tablespoon
margarine
or butter
½ teaspoon ground
cinnamon
¼ cup chopped
walnuts *or* pecans
1 cup all-purpose
flour
⅓ cup sugar
½ teaspoon baking
powder
¼ teaspoon baking
soda
Dash salt
1 egg
½ cup applesauce
¼ cup cooking oil
½ teaspoon vanilla

1 Turn oven to 350°. Put some shortening on a piece of paper towel or waxed paper. Spread the shortening over the bottom and sides of the baking pan to grease. Save until Step 5.

2 For the topping, in the small bowl put the brown sugar, margarine or butter, and cinnamon. Mix with the spoon or your hands till crumbly. Add nuts. Stir to mix. Put the topping on a piece of waxed paper. Save until Step 5.

3 In the large mixing bowl, put flour, sugar, baking powder, baking soda, and salt. Mix with the wooden spoon.

4 Crack the egg into the small mixing bowl. Beat the egg with the wooden spoon till the yolk and white are well mixed. Add the applesauce, cooking oil, and vanilla. Stir till mixed.

5 Add the applesauce mixture to the flour mixture. Stir till the dry ingredients are wet. Pour the batter into the greased pan. Use the rubber scraper to scrape all the batter from the bowl into the pan. Sprinkle the topping over the batter.

6 Put the pan in the oven. Bake for 20 to 25 minutes or till the toothpick comes out clean when inserted in the center of the cake. Turn off the oven. Use hot pads to remove the cake from the oven. Place the cake on the cooling rack. Cool about 15 minutes. Serve warm or cold. Serves 9.

Oatmeal Cinnamon Muffins

Look, kids! Oatmeal in a muffin instead of a bowl!

Equipment

Measuring cups
and spoons
12 paper bake cups
Muffin pan(s) for 12
muffins
Large mixing bowl
Wooden spoon
Table knife
Small mixing bowl
Fork
Large spoon
Hot pads

Ingredients

1⅓ cups all-purpose
flour
¾ cup quick-cooking
rolled oats
⅓ cup packed brown
sugar
2 teaspoons baking
powder
¼ teaspoon salt
¼ teaspoon ground
cinnamon
1 egg
¾ cup milk
¼ cup cooking oil
½ cup mixed dried
fruit bits
or raisins
Margarine *or* butter
(if you like)

1 Turn the oven to 400°. Put a paper bake cup into each of the muffin pan cups.

2 In the large mixing bowl put the flour, oats, brown sugar, baking powder, salt, and cinnamon. Stir with the wooden spoon to mix. Save until Step 4.

3 Crack the egg into the small mixing bowl. Beat the egg with the fork till the yolk and white are mixed. Add milk and oil to egg. Beat till well mixed. Stir in fruit bits or raisins.

4 Add the egg mixture to the flour mixture. Stir with the wooden spoon till the dry ingredients are wet. (The batter should be lumpy.) Use the large spoon to put the batter into muffin cups. Fill each muffin cup two-thirds full.

5 Put the muffin pan(s) in the oven. Bake for 20 to 25 minutes or till the muffins are golden. Turn off the oven.

6 Use hot pads to remove the muffin pan(s) from the oven. Tip the muffin pan(s) to remove the muffins. Cool about 5 minutes. Serve muffins warm with margarine or butter, if you like. Makes 12.

Early Bird's Breakfast

Start your day off on the right foot by making breakfast for your family.

Cool and Creamy Fruit Cup
Apple Snapple Oatmeal
Bakery or frozen muffins
Milk

Apple Snapple Oatmeal

Cool and Creamy Fruit Cup

Breakfast Countdown

Making this breakfast is easy, if you follow these steps.

1 If you are using frozen muffins, turn the oven to 350° for the muffins. (Bakery muffins don't need heating.)

2 Put all the equipment and ingredients needed for each recipe on the counter.

3 Put the muffins in the oven to heat for 18 to 20 minutes. Set a timer to let you know when they are done.

4 Make the Cool and Creamy Fruit Cup. Place it in the refrigerator while you make the oatmeal.

5 Make the Apple Snapple Oatmeal.

6 Dig in!

Cool and Creamy Fruit Cup

A sweet-and-tangy fruit and yogurt combo.

Equipment	Ingredients
Measuring cups Colander Medium mixing bowl Can opener Wooden spoon 4 small bowls	1 11-ounce can mandarin orange sections 1 8-ounce can pineapple tidbits (juice pack) 1 cup red *or* green seedless grapes 1 8-ounce carton lemon *or* orange yogurt

1 Put the colander in the mixing bowl. Empty the orange sections and pineapple tidbits into the colander letting the juices run into the bowl. Throw away the juices.

2 Put the drained fruit into the mixing bowl. Add the grapes. With the wooden spoon, gently stir the yogurt into the fruit. Spoon into the small bowls. Makes 4 servings.

Apple Snapple Oatmeal

Apple, raisins, and cinnamon are scrumptious additions to oatmeal.

Equipment

Measuring cups
  and spoons
Cutting board
Sharp knife
Large saucepan
Wooden spoon
Large spoon
4 cereal bowls

Ingredients

1 medium apple
  or **pear**
3 cups apple juice
  or **cider**
1⅓ cups regular rolled
  oats
¼ cup raisins *or*
  chopped pitted
  dates
¼ teaspoon ground
  cinnamon
  Milk
  Brown sugar
  (if you like)

1 On the cutting board, use the sharp knife to cut the apple or pear into 4 pieces. Cut out the core and throw it away. Chop each piece.

2 In the saucepan, put the chopped apple or pear, apple juice or cider, oats, raisins or dates, and cinnamon. Stir with the wooden spoon to mix. Put the pan on the burner. Turn the burner to medium-high heat. Cook just till bubbly. Turn burner to low. Simmer, uncovered, for 5 minutes, stirring now and then. Turn off the burner. Remove the saucepan from the burner.

3 With the large spoon, put the oatmeal into the cereal bowls. Serve immediately with milk and brown sugar, if you like. Makes 4 servings.

Microwave Directions

Prepare as above, *except* use *2½ cups* of apple juice or cider. Follow Step 1. In a *microwave-safe 2-quart casserole* put the chopped apple or pear, apple juice or cider, oats, raisins or dates, and cinnamon. Cover with the lid. Place in the microwave oven. Set on high (100%) power. Micro-cook for 3 minutes. Stir using the wooden spoon. Micro-cook, covered, on high for 3 to 4 minutes more or till hot and bubbly. Follow Step 3.

Bread Spreads

Make these great-tasting bread fix-ups to eat as snacks or with your breakfast.

Split and toast an *English muffin*. Spread generously with *American cheese spread*. Top with one or two drained, canned *pear* or *peach slices* or *pineapple cubes*.

Toast a *frozen waffle*. Spread with *peanut butter* and sprinkle with *miniature semisweet chocolate pieces*.

Toast a slice of *raisin bread.* Spread with *soft-style cream cheese* and your favorite *jelly or jam.*

Spread *peanut butter* over one 6- or 7-inch *flour tortilla.* Sprinkle with *sunflower nuts* or *mixed dried fruit bits.* Roll up.

Toast a sliced *bagel.* Spread one bagel half with *prepared mustard.* Top with a slice of *American cheese,* a slice of *ham,* and the other bagel half.

Nachos

Makes enough for you and three amigos (friends).

Equipment	Ingredients
Measuring cups and spoons 9-inch pie plate Small spoon Hot pads	20 tortilla chips 1 tablespoon salsa (if you like) ¼ cup shredded Monterey Jack, American, *or* cheddar cheese

1 Turn the oven to 350°. In the pie plate, arrange the tortilla chips in a single layer. Spoon a little salsa over each chip, if you like. Sprinkle chips with cheese.

2 Put the pie plate in the oven. Bake for 4 to 5 minutes or till the cheese melts. Use hot pads to remove the pie plate from the oven. Cool about 1 minute before eating. Makes 20 (4 servings).

 Microwave Directions

In a *microwave-safe 9-inch pie plate* arrange the tortilla chips in a single layer. Spoon a little salsa over each chip, if you like. Sprinkle with cheese.

Place in the microwave oven. Set on high (100%) power. Micro-cook for 30 to 40 seconds or till the cheese is melted. Cool about 1 minute.

Just-My-Size Pizzas

These were a favorite among our kid-testers, so we pictured them on the cover.

Equipment	Ingredients
Measuring cups	Shortening
Waxed paper *or* paper towel	1 10-ounce package refrigerated pizza dough
Baking sheet	1 8-ounce can pizza sauce
Kitchen scissors *or* pizza cutter	2 ounces sliced pepperoni
Can opener	¼ cup sliced pitted black olives
Small spoon	¼ cup chopped green pepper
Hot pads	1 4-ounce package (1 cup) shredded mozzarella cheese
Pancake turner	

1 Turn the oven to 425°. Put some shortening on a piece of waxed paper or paper towel. Spread the shortening over the baking sheet.

2 Unroll the pizza dough onto the baking sheet. Use the kitchen scissors or pizza cutter to cut the dough in half. Then, cut each half into 6 rectangles. Separate the rectangles on the baking sheet, leaving some space between them.

3 Spoon pizza sauce over each rectangle. Use the back of the spoon to spread the sauce over the dough. Top with pepperoni, olives, and green pepper. Sprinkle with cheese.

4 Put the pan in the oven. Bake for 10 to 12 minutes or till the crust is brown. Use hot pads to remove the pan from the oven. Turn off the oven. Use the pancake turner to remove the pizzas from the pan. Let the pizzas cool a few minutes before eating. Makes 12.

Your Microwave Oven

Microwave ovens are not all the same. Before you make a recipe in your microwave oven, ask your Mom or Dad how many watts it has. We tested our recipes in 600- to 700-watt microwave ovens. If yours has fewer watts, food may take a little longer to cook.

Peanut Butter Surprise Balls

Whip up these snacks when it's your turn to take treats to school.

Equipment

Measuring cups
and spoons
Medium mixing bowl
Wooden spoon
Plastic bag
Waxed paper
Small spoon
Container with a
tight cover

Ingredients

½ cup peanut butter
1 tablespoon honey
⅓ cup nonfat dry milk
powder
2 tablespoons sesame
seed
2 tablespoons toasted
wheat germ
½ cup cornflakes
Raisins, peanuts,
semisweet
chocolate pieces,
or candy-coated
milk chocolate
pieces

1 To make the dough, put peanut butter and honey in the bowl. Use the wooden spoon to stir till well mixed.

2 Add the dry milk powder, sesame seed, and wheat germ. Stir till well mixed.

3 Put the cornflakes in the plastic bag. Seal or tie the plastic bag shut. Crumple the bag, then use your hands to crush the cornflakes. Sprinkle the crushed cornflakes over a sheet of waxed paper.

4 Use the small spoon to scoop out a spoonful of the dough. Shape the dough around a raisin, peanut, chocolate piece, or candy. Roll in cornflake crumbs. Make more balls till all the ingredients are gone.

5 To store, put the snacks in the container. Cover the container tightly and put in the refrigerator. Makes about 25.

Banana-Berry Drink

A great-tasting snack to sip.

Equipment	Ingredients

Measuring cups
Table knife
Electric blender
2 tall glasses
	1 ripe medium
	  banana
	1 cup milk
	½ cup strawberry
	  yogurt
	4 ice cubes

1 Remove the peel from the banana. Use the table knife to cut the banana into chunks.

2 In the blender container put milk, yogurt, ice cubes, and banana. Cover with the lid. Blend about ½ minute or till smooth. Turn the blender off. Pour the drink into the glasses. Serve with strawberries, if you like. Makes 2 servings.

Milk Shakes

Make either chocolate or vanilla shakes by choosing different ice cream.

Equipment	Ingredients

Measuring cups
Electric blender
Ice cream scoop
   or large spoon
Rubber scraper
2 tall glasses
	¾ cup milk
	2 cups vanilla *or*
	    chocolate ice
	    cream

1 Pour milk into the blender container. Add *half* of the ice cream. Cover with the lid. Blend till smooth. Stop and scrape the sides using the rubber scraper, as needed.

2 Add the rest of the ice cream. Cover and blend just till smooth, stopping and scraping as needed. Pour into glasses. Makes 2 servings.

More Shakes

Banana Shakes: Make the shakes as directed above, *except* add *half* a *banana* each time you add ice cream (use one whole banana).

Peanut Butter Shakes: Make the shakes as directed above, *except* add 2 tablespoons *peanut butter* to the milk.

Malted Milk Shakes: Make the shakes as directed above, *except* add 2 tablespoons *instant malted milk powder* to the milk.

Honey Limeade

A refreshing drink on a hot day.

Equipment	Ingredients
Measuring cups and spoons Large pitcher Large spoon 6 tall glasses	1 cup reconstituted lime juice 5 cups water ⅔ cup sugar 2 tablespoons honey Ice cubes

1 Put the lime juice in the pitcher. Add the water, sugar, and honey. Stir till the sugar is dissolved. Put in the refrigerator till serving time.

2 Put several ice cubes in each glass. Pour limeade over the ice cubes in the glasses. Makes 6 (8-ounce) servings.

Shake-a-Snack

Equipment	Ingredients
Measuring cups Plastic bag	1 cup candy-coated, fruit-flavored pieces *or* candy-coated, milk chocolate pieces 1 cup peanuts 1 cup raisins

1 In the plastic bag, put the candy, peanuts, and raisins. Close the bag tightly. Shake well to mix.

2 Store the mix in the plastic bag for up to 2 weeks. Makes 3 cups (24 servings).

Fruit Lover's Pops

"Tastes better than the kind you buy at the store," Dennis, our kid-tester, told us.

Equipment

Measuring cups
10 3-ounce paper cups
13x9x2-inch baking pan
Medium saucepan
Wooden spoon
Can opener
Kitchen scissors
Ruler
Foil
Sharp knife
10 wooden sticks

Ingredients

1 3-ounce package fruit-flavored gelatin (any flavor)
1 cup water
1 6-ounce can frozen apple, orange, *or* pineapple juice concentrate
1 cup cold water

1 Put the paper cups in the baking pan. Save until Step 4.

2 In the medium saucepan combine the fruit-flavored gelatin and 1 cup water. Put the saucepan on a burner. Turn the burner to high. Cook and stir with the wooden spoon till the mixture is bubbly. Turn off the burner. Remove the saucepan from the burner.

3 Add the frozen fruit juice concentrate. Stir with the wooden spoon until the juice concentrate is melted. Stir in 1 cup cold water.

4 Pour the juice mixture into the liquid measuring cup. Then, pour the juice mixture into the paper cups. Using the scissors and the ruler, cut ten 4-inch squares from the foil. Carefully cover each paper cup with a foil square. Use the knife to make a slit in the center of each foil top. Push a wooden stick through the hole into the juice mixture. Put the pops in the freezer. Freeze about 6 hours or till firm.

5 To serve, remove the desired number of pops from the freezer. Let stand at room temperature about 5 minutes. Peel off the foil and the paper cups. Makes 10.

Strawberry Pink Shakes

Buy a pint of ice cream for easy measuring.

Equipment	Ingredients

Medium mixing bowl
Measuring cups
Electric blender
Ice cream scoop
  or large spoon
Rubber scraper
3 *or* 4 tall glasses
	1 10-ounce package
	     frozen
	     strawberries
	1 cup milk
	2 cups strawberry ice
	    cream *or*
	    strawberry frozen
	    yogurt

1 To thaw strawberries, fill the mixing bowl with warm tap water. Place the unwrapped package of strawberries in the water. Let stand 10 minutes or till the strawberries are thawed.

2 Put strawberries and their juice into the blender container. Cover with the lid and blend till smooth. Add the milk. Cover and blend till smooth again.

3 Scoop or spoon *half* of the ice cream or yogurt into the strawberry mixture in the blender container. Cover and blend till smooth. Turn off the blender and scrape the sides with a rubber scraper, as needed. Add the rest of the ice cream or yogurt. Cover and blend just till smooth, stopping the blender and scraping as needed. Pour into glasses. Makes 3 or 4 servings.

29

Jack-O'-Lantern Loaf

Pumpkin gives this bread its name.

Equipment	Ingredients
Measuring cups and spoons	Shortening
Paper towel *or* waxed paper	2 cups all-purpose flour
9x5x3-inch loaf pan	2 teaspoons baking powder
Medium mixing bowl	½ teaspoon pumpkin pie spice
Wooden spoon	¼ teaspoon salt
Large mixing bowl	¼ teaspoon baking soda
Table knife	1 cup packed brown sugar
Custard cup *or* small bowl	⅓ cup shortening
Can opener	2 eggs
Rubber scraper	1 cup canned pumpkin
Wooden toothpick	¼ cup milk
Hot pads	½ cup broken pecans *or* walnuts (if you like)
Cooling rack	

1 Turn oven to 350°. Put some shortening on a piece of paper towel or waxed paper. Spread the shortening over the bottom and sides of the loaf pan to grease. Save till Step 5.

2 In the medium mixing bowl, put flour, baking powder, pumpkin pie spice, salt, and baking soda. Stir with the wooden spoon. Save till Step 5.

3 In the large mixing bowl, put the brown sugar and ⅓ cup shortening. Stir with the wooden spoon till well mixed.

4 Crack *one* egg into the custard cup. Add the egg to the brown sugar mixture. Stir till well mixed. Repeat with remaining egg. Add the pumpkin and milk to brown sugar mixture. Stir till mixed.

5 Add the flour mixture to the pumpkin mixture. Stir till smooth. Stir in nuts, if you like. Spoon the batter into the greased pan. Use the rubber scraper to scrape all the batter from the bowl into the pan. Spread batter evenly in the pan.

6 Put the pan in the oven. Bake about 1 hour or till the toothpick comes out clean when inserted in the center of the loaf. Turn off oven. Use hot pads to remove the loaf from oven. Cool in pan on the cooling rack for 10 minutes. Turn the pan upside down on rack. Lift pan from loaf. Turn the loaf right side up on the rack. Cool before slicing. Makes 1 loaf (18 servings).

Pop-and-Crunch Snack Mix

A great snack to munch while watching TV or reading a book.

Equipment

Measuring cups and
  spoons
Small saucepan
Wooden spoon
Large mixing bowl
Container with tight
  cover

Ingredients

3 tablespoons
  margarine
  or butter
½ teaspoon apple
  pie spice
2 cups oyster
  crackers
4 cups popped
  popcorn
1 cup dry roasted
  peanuts
3 0.9-ounce envelopes
  mixed chewy fruit
  bits *or* cherry,
  grape, strawberry,
  or orange chewy
  fruit bits

1 Put the margarine or butter in the small saucepan. Put the saucepan on a burner. Turn the burner to low. Heat till the margarine is melted. Turn off the burner. Remove the saucepan from the burner. Add apple pie spice. Stir with the wooden spoon to mix.

2 Place the oyster crackers in the mixing bowl. Pour the melted margarine mixture over the oyster crackers. Stir till crackers are well coated with the margarine mixture.

3 Add popcorn, peanuts, and fruit bits. Stir with the wooden spoon or your hands till mixed. To store, put the mix in the container. Cover tightly. Store up to 1 week. Makes 8 cups (16 servings).

 Microwave Directions

Place margarine or butter in a *microwave-safe 1-cup measuring cup or custard cup.* Put the cup in the microwave oven. Set on high (100%) power. Micro-cook for 40 to 50 seconds or till margarine is melted. Stir in apple pie spice. Follow Steps 2 and 3 as directed above.

Cocoa-on-Call

This cocoa mix makes an extra chocolaty drink.

Equipment	Ingredients

Measuring cups
Storage container
  with airtight cover
Wooden spoon
Mug
Small saucepan
Small spoon
	2½ cups nonfat dry
	    milk powder
	1 cup powdered
	   sugar
	½ cup unsweetened
	   cocoa powder
	Water
	Marshmallows
	   (if you like)

1 To make the cocoa mix, in the storage container put dry milk powder, powdered sugar, and cocoa powder. Stir with the wooden spoon till mixed. Cover the container. Store the cocoa mix in a cool, dry place.

2 For each serving, put ⅓ cup of the cocoa mix in a mug. Put ⅔ cup *water* in the saucepan. Put the pan on burner. Turn to high. Heat till the water is bubbly. Turn off the burner. Carefully pour the hot water into the mug. Stir with the small spoon till mixed. Top with marshmallows, if you like. Makes enough mix for 10 (6-ounce) servings.

 Microwave Directions

Make the cocoa mix as directed in Step 1. For each serving, put ⅓ cup of the cocoa mix in a *microwave-safe mug*. Add ⅔ cup cold *water*. Stir with the small spoon till mixed. Put the mug in the microwave oven. Set on high (100%) power. Micro-cook for 30 seconds. Stir. If the cocoa is not hot enough, micro-cook for 15 to 30 seconds more.

Milk Chocolate Bubble Ring

Each sugar-and-cinnamon-coated bread bubble holds a chocolate surprise.

Equipment

Measuring cups
and spoons
Paper towel *or*
waxed paper
6½-cup ovenproof
ring mold
Small saucepan
Ruler
Small mixing bowl
Wooden spoon
Hot pads
Cooling rack
Large plate

Ingredients

Shortening
20 milk chocolate
kisses
¼ cup margarine
or butter
2 packages (10 each)
refrigerated
biscuits
½ cup sugar
½ teaspoon ground
cinnamon

1 Turn the oven to 375°. Put some shortening on a piece of paper towel or waxed paper. Spread the shortening over the inside of the ring mold. Save till Step 6. Unwrap the chocolate kisses. Save till Step 4.

2 Put margarine or butter in the saucepan. Put on a burner. Turn burner to low. Heat till margarine melts. Turn off the burner. Remove the pan from burner. Save till Step 5.

3 Separate the biscuits. Flatten each biscuit into a 3-inch circle.

4 Place a chocolate kiss in the center of a biscuit. Wrap the biscuit around chocolate forming a ball. Pinch edges to seal firmly. Repeat with remaining chocolate kisses and biscuits.

5 In the bowl, mix the sugar and cinnamon. Dip each ball in the margarine. Then, roll in sugar-cinnamon mixture.

6 Arrange the balls in the greased ring mold. Form two layers, placing the balls of dough in the second layer between the balls of dough in the first layer.

7 Put the ring mold in the oven. Bake about 20 minutes or till the bubble ring is golden. Turn off the oven. Using hot pads, remove the mold from oven. Put it on cooling rack. Cool about 1 minute. Turn mold upside down on plate. Remove the ring mold. Cool about 10 minutes. Serve warm. Serves 10.

Fruit Fix-Ups

Turn snack time into fruit time with these luscious ideas for dressing up apples, bananas, and other fruits.

Stir together ½ cup *fudge ice cream topping* and ½ cup *strawberry* or *raspberry yogurt*. Dip *apple wedges, orange slices,* or *strawberries* into the chocolate mixture.

Cut two *pineapple rings* in half. Place in a dessert dish. Use a small ice cream scoop to place three scoops of *cottage cheese* in a dish. Top with *maraschino cherries.*

To make a sea creature, line a plate with *lettuce leaves.* For the body, arrange drained, canned *peach* or *pear slices* on the lettuce. Add some fresh *apple slices* (brush the apple slices with a little lemon juice to keep them fresh, if you like). With a vegetable peeler, cut long thin strips of *carrot* for the tail. Use a little *soft-style cream cheese or peanut butter* to attach *raisins* for eyes. Slice a *maraschino cherry.* Cut one slice in half. Attach one half to the peach or pear for the mouth.

Slice *half* of a *banana.* Mix a single-serving can of *vanilla pudding,* ¼ cup thawed *frozen, whipped dessert topping,* and banana slices.

Sloppy Toms

Call them Sloppy Toms when you use turkey, and sloppy joes when you use beef.

Equipment

Measuring cups
and spoons
Large skillet
Wooden spoon
Colander
Medium mixing bowl
Can opener
Large spoon
Plates

Ingredients

1 pound ground raw
turkey *or* ground
beef
½ cup frozen chopped
onion
1 8-ounce can tomato
sauce
1 teaspoon chili
powder
1 teaspoon prepared
mustard
1 teaspoon
Worcestershire
sauce
8 hamburger buns,
split
1 4-ounce package
(1 cup) shredded
cheddar cheese

1 Use your hands to break up the ground turkey or beef as you put it in the skillet. Add onion to the skillet. Put the skillet on the burner. Turn the burner to medium-high. Cook, stirring with the wooden spoon, about 10 minutes or till there is no pink color left in the meat. Turn off the burner. Remove the skillet from the burner.

2 Place the colander over the mixing bowl. Spoon the meat mixture into the colander. Let fat drain into the bowl. Spoon the meat mixture back into the skillet. Put the fat in a container to throw away.

3 Stir tomato sauce, chili powder, mustard, and Worcestershire sauce into the meat mixture.

4 Put the skillet on a burner. Turn the burner to high. Cook till the meat mixture is bubbly, stirring now and then. Turn the burner to low. Simmer for 5 minutes, stirring now and then. Turn off the burner. Remove the skillet.

5 For each serving, put the bottom of a bun on a plate. Spoon some of the meat mixture over the bottom half of the bun. Sprinkle it with some of the shredded cheese. Cover with the bun top. Repeat for each sandwich. Makes 8.

Chicken Pocket Burgers

These chicken burgers taste great in hamburger buns, too.

Equipment	Ingredients
Measuring cups and spoons **Baking sheet** **Cutting board** **Sharp knife** **Kitchen scissors** **Small bowl** **Small spoon** **Hot pads** **Table knife** **Pancake turner**	**4 frozen breaded chicken patties** **1 large tomato** **2 large pita bread rounds** **¼ cup mayonnaise *or* salad dressing** **1 teaspoon sweet pickle relish** **4 lettuce leaves**

1 Place the frozen chicken patties on the baking sheet. Bake chicken patties according to the package directions.

2 While the chicken patties bake, put the tomato on the cutting board. Use the sharp knife to cut the tomato into thin slices. Use the scissors to cut the pita bread crosswise in half (so you have four half circles). Save until Step 5.

3 In the small bowl, put mayonnaise or salad dressing and pickle relish. Stir with the spoon till mixed.

4 When the chicken patties are done, use hot pads to remove the baking sheet from the oven. Turn off the oven. Spoon a little of the mayonnaise mixture on top of each patty.

5 Use the table knife to spread the remaining mayonnaise mixture over the inside of the pita bread halves.

6 For each serving, line one pita bread half with lettuce and sliced tomato. Use the pancake turner to put a chicken patty in the pita half. Repeat for each sandwich. Makes 4.

Pint-Sized Heros

We scaled down a hero sandwich to just your size.

Equipment

Cutting board
Sharp knife
Table knife

Ingredients

1 small tomato
Mayonnaise *or*
   salad dressing
   (if you like)
Prepared mustard
   (if you like)
4 hot dog buns, split
4 lettuce leaves
4 ounces sliced Swiss
   or American
   cheese
6 ounces sliced, fully
   cooked ham,
   turkey, *or*
   roast beef
2 ounces sliced
   salami *or* summer
   sausage

1 On the cutting board, use the sharp knife to cut the tomato into thin slices. Save them until Step 3.

2 Use the table knife to spread mayonnaise or salad dressing and mustard inside the buns, if you like.

3 Tear the lettuce leaves to fit the buns. Put lettuce on the bottom half of each bun. Then, top each with cheese; ham, turkey, or roast beef; and salami or summer sausage. Add tomato slices and bun tops. Makes 4.

Tuna Salad Sandwiches

For chicken salad sandwiches, use a 5-ounce can of chunk-style chicken instead of tuna.

Equipment
Measuring cups and spoons
Colander
Medium mixing bowl
Can opener
Fork
Small spoon
Table knife

Ingredients
1 6½- *or* 7-ounce can tuna
¼ cup mayonnaise *or* salad dressing
2 tablespoons sweet pickle *or* dill pickle relish
6 slices whole wheat *or* white bread
Lettuce leaves

1 To make the filling, place the colander over the mixing bowl. Empty the tuna into the colander so the liquid drains into the bowl. Throw away the liquid.

2 Put the drained tuna into the bowl. Break it into chunks with the fork. Stir in the mayonnaise or salad dressing and relish.

3 For each sandwich, spoon about *one-third* of the filling on *one* slice of bread. With a table knife, spread the filling to the edges of the bread. Tear lettuce leaves to fit the bread. Place some lettuce on top of the filling. Put another slice of bread on top. Cut in half. Repeat for each sandwich. Makes 3.

Hot Tuna Buns

Assemble the ingredients listed above, *except* for the lettuce and bread. Instead you'll need 3 *hamburger or hot dog buns* and 3 slices of *American cheese.* Turn the oven to 350°. Follow Steps 1 and 2. Spoon *one-third* of the filling on the bottom half of *each* bun. Tear cheese to fit buns. Place cheese on top of filling. Cover with bun tops. Wrap each sandwich in *foil.* Heat in the oven for 15 minutes.

Grilled Cheese and More

Charlie, our kid-tester, said this sandwich is tastier than a regular grilled cheese.

Equipment	Ingredients

Table knife
Small skillet
Pancake turner
	1 tablespoon
	   margarine *or*
	   butter
	2 slices white *or*
	   whole wheat
	   bread
	2 slices American,
	   Swiss, cheddar,
	   or Colby cheese
	1 thin slice fully
	   cooked ham,
	   chicken, *or*
	   turkey

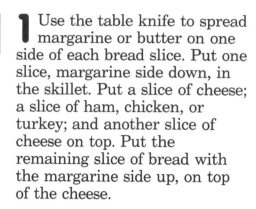

1 Use the table knife to spread margarine or butter on one side of each bread slice. Put one slice, margarine side down, in the skillet. Put a slice of cheese; a slice of ham, chicken, or turkey; and another slice of cheese on top. Put the remaining slice of bread with the margarine side up, on top of the cheese.

2 Put the skillet on a burner. Turn the burner to medium. Cook for 4 to 5 minutes or till the bottom side is toasted and golden. To check the bottom, lift the sandwich with the pancake turner and peek underneath.

3 With the pancake turner, turn the sandwich over. Cook the other side about 2 minutes or till it is toasted and golden. Turn off the burner. Remove the skillet. Lift the sandwich from the skillet with the pancake turner. Cut the sandwich in half. Makes 1.

Reuben-Style Pockets

Stuff corned beef, Swiss cheese, and pickles into pocket bread for this nifty sandwich.

Equipment	Ingredients
Kitchen scissors Table knife	2 **large pita bread rounds** **Thousand Island salad dressing** 2 **2½-ounce packages very thinly sliced corned beef** 4 **slices Swiss cheese** 4 **lettuce leaves** 8 **dill _or_ sweet pickle slices**

1 Use the scissors to cut each pita in half crosswise (so you have four half circles).

2 With the table knife, spread the inside of the pita pockets with salad dressing.

3 Put some of the corned beef in each pocket. Tear the cheese into pieces that will fit in the pockets. Add cheese, lettuce leaves, and pickle slices to each pocket. Makes 4.

Beef 'n' Slaw Pockets

Assemble the ingredients listed above, _except_ for the salad dressing. You also will need ½ cup _coleslaw_ (from a deli or deli section of your grocery store). Skip Step 2. Make sandwiches as directed in Steps 1 and 3. Then, spoon some coleslaw into each sandwich.

Taco Cheeseburgers

A chili-flavored cheeseburger served in a taco shell.

Equipment

Measuring spoons
Large mixing bowl
Waxed paper
Ruler
13x9x2-inch baking
  pan
Cutting board
Sharp knife
Table knife
Hot pads
Pancake turner

Ingredients

1 **pound ground beef**
2 **tablespoons taco
   sauce**
1½ **teaspoons chili
   powder**
¼ **teaspoon salt**
1 **medium tomato
   (if you like)**
4 **slices Monterey
   Jack *or* American
   cheese**
8 **taco shells**
8 **lettuce leaves**

1 Turn the oven to 350°. Use your hands to break up the ground beef as you put it into the mixing bowl. Add taco sauce, chili powder, and salt. Use your hands to mix well.

2 Place a sheet of waxed paper on the counter or table. Put the meat mixture on the waxed paper. Divide the meat mixture into 8 portions. Shape each portion into an oval patty, about ½ inch thick.

3 Place the patties in the baking pan. Put the pan in the oven. Bake for 15 minutes.

4 While the patties are cooking, put the tomato on the cutting board. Cut it in half with the sharp knife. Chop each half into small pieces. Save until Step 7.

5 With the table knife, cut each cheese slice diagonally in half to form 2 triangles.

6 Use the hot pads to remove the pan from the oven. Place 1 cheese triangle on each patty. Put the pan back in the oven for 1 to 2 minutes or till the cheese melts. Turn off the oven. Remove the pan from the oven.

7 Use the pancake turner to put a patty in a taco shell. Add a lettuce leaf and some chopped tomato. Serve with additional taco sauce, if you like. Repeat for each sandwich. Makes 8.

All-American Hamburgers

A frequent star at lunch and dinner tables.

Equipment

Waxed paper
Ruler
Large skillet
Pancake turner

Ingredients

1 **pound ground beef**
 Salt
 Pepper
4 **hamburger buns,**
   split
 Catsup, mustard,
   lettuce leaves,
   ***and/or* dill pickle**
   ***or* sweet pickle**
   slices (if you like)

1 Place a piece of waxed paper on the counter or table. Put the ground beef on the waxed paper. Use your hands to divide the meat into 4 portions. Shape each portion into a flat, round patty, about 3½ inches in diameter. Put the hamburger patties in the skillet.

2 Put the skillet on a burner. Turn the burner to medium. Cook about 7 minutes or till the patties are brown on the bottom. To check, lift the patties with the pancake turner and peek underneath.

3 With the pancake turner, turn each patty over. Sprinkle the patties with salt and pepper. Cook about 4 minutes or till the bottoms of patties are brown. Turn off the burner. Remove the skillet from the burner.

4 With the pancake turner, lift each patty from the skillet. Put each hamburger in a split bun. Serve with catsup, mustard, lettuce, and pickle slices, if you like. Makes 4.

Cheeseburgers

You will need 2 slices of *American cheese*. Cut each cheese slice diagonally into 2 triangles. Follow Steps 1, 2, and 3. Then, put a cheese triangle on top of each burger. Put the lid on the skillet. Let stand 1 minute. Serve as directed in Step 4.

Backyard Lunch

Invite three of your friends over for lunch. Turn it into a picnic by eating your sandwich, vegetables, and dip in the backyard.

Chicken Club Croissants
Dip-It Sauce with Vegetables
Milk
Cookies

Chicken Club Croissants

Dip-It Sauce with Vegetables

Lunch Countdown

Follow these simple steps and lunch will be ready before you know it.

1 Make the Dip-It Sauce with Vegetables. Put the sauce and vegetables in the refrigerator to keep them cold.

2 Make the Chicken Club Croissants. Put them on plates.

3 Serve the Dip-It-Sauce with Vegetables. Pour the milk in glasses. Arrange the cookies on a plate.

Chicken Club Croissants

Croissants dress up these chicken and tomato sandwiches.

Equipment	Ingredients
Sharp knife Table knife Cutting board	4 croissants *or* hamburger buns 2 tablespoons creamy bacon, buttermilk, *or* other creamy salad dressing 1 small tomato 4 lettuce leaves 4 ounces sliced, cooked chicken *or* turkey 4 ounces sliced Swiss *or* American cheese

1 Cut the croissants or buns in half horizontally with the sharp knife. With the table knife, spread the cut sides with some of the salad dressing.

2 On the cutting board, thinly slice the tomato with the sharp knife. Tear the lettuce leaves to fit the croissants or hamburger buns.

3 On the bottom half of each croissant or hamburger bun, place lettuce, chicken or turkey, and cheese. Top each with a tomato slice and the top half of the croissant or bun. Makes 4.

Dip-It Sauce with Vegetables

Save any leftovers for snack time.

Equipment

Measuring cups
  and spoons
Strainer
Medium mixing bowl
Wooden spoon
Clear plastic wrap
Cutting board
Sharp knife
Large mixing bowl
Small serving bowl
Serving platter

Ingredients

1 cup cream-style
    cottage cheese
½ of an 8-ounce
    container soft-
    style cream
    cheese with onion
    and chives
1 teaspoon dried
    dillweed
  Celery, carrots,
    cauliflower, *and*
    broccoli

1 Place the strainer over the medium mixing bowl. Put the cottage cheese in the strainer. Let the liquid run into the bowl. Lift the strainer from the bowl. Throw away the liquid.

2 Put the drained cottage cheese in the mixing bowl. Add the cream cheese and dillweed. Stir with the wooden spoon till well mixed. Cover with plastic wrap. Put in the refrigerator till serving time.

3 Wash the celery, carrots, cauliflower, and broccoli. On the cutting board, cut celery and carrots into 2- or 3-inch lengths with the sharp knife. Cut any thick pieces of carrot in half lengthwise. For cauliflower and broccoli, break off small bite-size buds. Put the vegetables in the large mixing bowl. Add enough cold water to cover the vegetables. (This keeps them crisp till serving time.) Put the vegetables in the refrigerator.

4 To serve, drain the vegetables in the strainer. Put the cheese mixture in the serving bowl. Arrange the vegetables on the serving platter. To eat, dip the vegetables into the cheese mixture. Makes 4 servings.

Chicken Chow Mein

Our kid-tester, Heather, liked the crunchy water chestnuts in the stir-fry vegetables.

Equipment	Ingredients
Measuring cups and spoons Large saucepan with lid Wooden spoon Small mixing bowl 4 plates	1½ cups chopped cooked chicken 1 10-ounce package frozen stir-fry vegetables with seasonings ¼ cup water ¼ teaspoon ground ginger ½ cup orange juice 2 teaspoons cornstarch 1 3-ounce can chow mein noodles

1 In the saucepan, put chicken, vegetables with seasoning, water, and ginger. Stir with the wooden spoon.

2 Put the saucepan on a burner. Turn the burner to medium-high. Cook till bubbly. Cover saucepan. Turn burner to low. Cook 5 minutes or till vegetables are crisp-tender.

3 In the bowl, put orange juice and cornstarch. Stir to mix. Stir juice mixture into chicken mixture. Cook and stir till thick and bubbly. Then, cook and stir for 2 minutes more. Turn off the burner. Remove saucepan.

4 For each serving, arrange *one-fourth* of the chow mein noodles on *each* plate. Spoon the chicken mixture over the noodles. Makes 4 servings.

Microwave Directions

In a *microwave-safe 2-quart casserole*, put chicken, vegetables with seasoning, water, and ginger. Stir with the spoon. Cover casserole. Place in microwave oven. Set on high (100%) power. Micro-cook 5 minutes. Stir.

In the bowl, put orange juice and cornstarch. Stir to mix. Stir juice mixture into chicken mixture. Cook for 5 to 8 minutes more or till thick and bubbly. Follow Step 4.

First-Place Crispy Chicken

Potato chips and rice cereal coat this juicy oven-fried chicken.

Equipment	Ingredients
Measuring cups and spoons Paper towels Plastic bag Rolling pin 9-inch pie plate Small spoon Table knife Shallow mixing bowl 15x10x1-inch baking pan Hot pads	2 pounds meaty chicken pieces (breasts, thighs, and drumsticks) 2 cups potato chips 1½ cups crisp rice cereal Dash pepper 1 egg 2 tablespoons milk

1 Turn the oven to 375°. Remove the skin from the chicken, if you like. To skin chicken, pull the skin away from the meat. Rinse the chicken under cold water. Pat dry with paper towels. Save until Step 4.

2 In the plastic bag, put the potato chips and cereal. Seal or tie the plastic bag shut. Use the rolling pin to crush the chips and cereal. Pour the crumbs into the pie plate. Add pepper. Stir to mix using the small spoon. Save until Step 4.

3 Crack the egg into the mixing bowl. With the small spoon or a fork, beat lightly till the white and yolk are mixed. Add the milk. Stir to mix.

4 Dip each piece of chicken in the egg mixture. Turn to coat both sides. Then, roll each chicken piece in the crumb mixture. Press the crumbs against the chicken so they stick. Place chicken, meaty-side up, in the baking pan. Sprinkle with any remaining crumbs.

5 Put the pan in the oven. Bake 45 to 55 minutes or till no pink color is left in the chicken. To see if chicken is done, remove a piece of chicken and cut into it. Turn off the oven. Use hot pads to remove the pan from the oven. Serves 4.

Chili-on-Muffins

For spicy hot chili, use 2 teaspoons of chili powder. Use less for a milder flavor.

Equipment

Measuring cups
and spoons
Large skillet
Wooden spoon
Colander
Medium mixing bowl
Can opener
4 plates
Table knife
Small spoon

Ingredients

4 frozen corn muffins
½ pound ground beef
1 15¾-ounce can chili
  beans with chili
  gravy
1 8-ounce can stewed
  tomatoes
1 cup frozen whole
  kernel corn
1 to 2 teaspoons chili
  powder
4 slices American
  cheese
½ of an 8-ounce
  container sour
  cream dip with
  toasted onion
  (if you like)

1 Thaw muffins according to package directions.

2 While muffins thaw, use your hands to break up the ground beef as you put it in the skillet. Put the skillet on a burner. Turn the burner to medium-high. Cook, stirring with the wooden spoon, till no pink color is left in the meat. Turn off the burner. Remove the skillet from the burner.

3 Place the colander over the bowl. Spoon the meat into the colander. Let the fat drain into the bowl. Spoon the meat back into the skillet. Put the fat in a container to throw away.

4 Stir the *undrained* beans, *undrained* tomatoes, corn, and chili powder into the meat. Turn the burner to medium-high. Heat till bubbly. Turn the burner to low. Simmer, uncovered, about 5 minutes or till corn is tender and mixture is thick. Stir now and then.

5 While the meat mixture cooks, break corn muffins in half. Place a muffin on each plate. Using the table knife, cut cheese slices diagonally in half to make triangles.

6 Spoon the meat mixture over each muffin. Top each muffin with cheese triangles. If you like, spoon some sour cream dip on top. Makes 4 servings.

Taco Flats

Some kid-testers scooped up this spicy meat sauce with the chips instead of their forks.

Equipment

Measuring cups
Paper towels
Large skillet
Wooden spoon
Colander
Medium mixing bowl
Can opener
4 plates
Small spoon

Ingredients

½ head of lettuce
1 pound ground beef
½ cup frozen chopped onion
1 8-ounce can tomato sauce
1 8-ounce jar taco sauce
4 cups tortilla chips
1 4-ounce package (1 cup) shredded Monterey Jack *or* cheddar cheese
Dairy sour cream (if you like)
Taco sauce (if you like)

1 Rinse the lettuce under cold running water. Separate it into leaves. Put it on paper towels to drain. Pat it dry with more paper towels. Tear it into bite-size pieces. Save until Step 5.

2 Use your hands to break up the ground beef as you put it in the skillet. Add the onion. Put the skillet on the burner. Turn burner to medium-high. Cook, stirring with the wooden spoon, till there is no pink color left in the meat. Turn off the burner. Remove the skillet from burner.

3 Place the colander over the mixing bowl. Spoon the meat mixture into the colander. Let the fat drain into the bowl. Spoon the meat and onion back into the skillet. Put the fat in a container to throw away.

4 Stir the tomato sauce and jar of taco sauce into the meat mixture. Put the skillet back on the burner. Turn the burner to medium-high. Cook till bubbly. Turn the burner to low. Simmer, uncovered, about 10 minutes or till the mixture is thick. Stir now and then. Turn off the burner. Remove the skillet from the burner.

5 Arrange tortilla chips on the plates. Arrange lettuce over chips. Spoon the meat mixture over the lettuce. Sprinkle the meat mixture with cheese. Spoon sour cream and more taco sauce on top, if you like. Makes 4 servings.

Seafood Salad

You can use either crab-flavored fish or shrimp in this salad.

Equipment	Ingredients
Measuring cups Large mixing bowl Colander Paper towels Medium mixing bowl Can opener 4 salad plates Small spoon	1 8-ounce package frozen, crab-flavored, salad-style fish *or* frozen, peeled, cooked shrimp 1 6-ounce package frozen pea pods ½ small head of lettuce 1 8-ounce can sliced water chestnuts ½ cup seasoned croutons ¼ cup grated Parmesan cheese ¼ cup Thousand Island *or* French salad dressing

1 In the large bowl, put the inner package of crab-flavored fish or the package of shrimp. Fill the bowl with cold water. Let stand for 30 minutes.

2 While the fish is thawing, put the pea pods in the colander. Place the colander in the sink. Run cold water over the pea pods till they are thawed. Place pea pods on paper towels. Save until Step 5.

3 Rinse the lettuce under cold running water. Separate it into leaves. Put it on paper towels to drain. Pat the lettuce dry with more paper towels. Tear it into bite-size pieces. Save until Step 5.

4 Put the colander over the medium bowl. Empty the water chestnuts into the colander, letting the liquid run into the bowl. Throw away the liquid. Save *half* of the water chestnuts until Step 5. (Put remaining water chestnuts in an airtight container and place in the refrigerator to use another time.)

5 Divide the lettuce evenly among the salad plates. Arrange crab-flavored fish, pea pods, and water chestnuts on top. Sprinkle with croutons and Parmesan cheese. Before serving, spoon salad dressing on top. Makes 4 servings.

Super Supper Salad

Toss together a meal in a salad bowl.

Equipment	Ingredients
Measuring cups and spoons Paper towels Large salad bowl Colander	½ head of lettuce 12 cherry tomatoes ½ cup alfalfa *or* bean sprouts (if you like) 1 2½- *or* 3-ounce package very thinly sliced, fully cooked ham 1 2½- *or* 3-ounce package very thinly sliced, cooked chicken *or* turkey 6 slices American *or* process Swiss cheese 2 tablespoons cooked bacon pieces French, Italian, *or* other salad dressing

1 Rinse lettuce under cold running water. Separate it into leaves. Put it on paper towels to drain. Pat lettuce dry with more paper towels. Tear it into bite-size pieces and put it in the salad bowl.

2 Rinse the cherry tomatoes under cold running water. Remove any green stems from the tomatoes. Add them to the salad bowl.

3 Put the sprouts in the colander. Rinse them under cold running water. Place the sprouts on paper towels. Pat them dry with more paper towels. Sprinkle the sprouts over the lettuce and tomatoes.

4 Tear the ham, chicken or turkey, and cheese into bite-size pieces. Add them to the salad bowl. Sprinkle the salad with bacon pieces. To toss the salad, pick up the salad ingredients with your hands, reaching to the bottom of the bowl. Drop the ingredients back into the bowl. Repeat till everything is well mixed. Serve with your favorite salad dressing. Makes 4 servings.

Chicken and Biscuit Dinners

Everyone gets his or her own.

Equipment

Measuring cups
and spoons
Kitchen scissors
Medium saucepan
Wooden spoon
4 small casseroles *or*
10-ounce custard
cups
Shallow baking pan
Ladle *or* large spoon
Hot pads

Ingredients

1 package (6)
refrigerated
biscuits
1½ cups chopped,
cooked chicken
or turkey
1 12-ounce jar
chicken *or* turkey
gravy
1 cup frozen cut
green beans
or peas
¼ teaspoon poultry
seasoning
Dash pepper

1 Turn the oven to 350°. Using the scissors, cut each biscuit in half. Save until Step 3.

2 In the saucepan, put the chicken or turkey, gravy, green beans or peas, poultry seasoning, and pepper. Mix together with the wooden spoon. Put the saucepan on the burner. Turn the burner to medium. Cook and stir till bubbly. Turn off the burner. Remove the saucepan from the burner.

3 Put the casseroles or custard cups in the baking pan. Use the ladle or large spoon to spoon the hot chicken mixture into each casserole. Put *three* biscuit pieces on top of *each* casserole.

4 Put the pan with the casseroles in the oven. Bake for 15 to 18 minutes or till the biscuits are golden. Use hot pads to remove the baking pan from the oven. Turn off the oven. Makes 4 servings.

Hot Dog! It's Macaroni!

Macaroni + cheese + hot dogs = delicious eating.

Equipment	Ingredients

Measuring cups
Cutting board
Table knife
Large saucepan
Colander
Wooden spoon
	1 8-ounce package
	   chicken, turkey,
	   or beef hot dogs
	8 ounces American
	   cheese slices
	1 cup corkscrew *or*
	   elbow macaroni
	1½ cups frozen peas *or*
	   mixed vegetables
	1 cup milk

1 On the cutting board, use the table knife to cut the hot dogs into bite-size pieces. Tear the cheese slices into small pieces. Save until Step 3.

2 In the saucepan, cook the macaroni according to the package directions. Turn off the burner. Remove the saucepan from the burner. Place the colander in the sink. Carefully pour the contents of the pan into the colander.

3 Return the warm macaroni to the saucepan. Use the wooden spoon to stir in the hot dogs, cheese, peas or mixed vegetables, and milk. Place the saucepan on a burner. Turn the burner to medium. Cook and stir about 10 minutes or till the cheese is melted. Turn off the burner. Remove the saucepan from the burner. Serves 4.

Turkey Mini Loaves

Melted cheese oozes from the center of each little loaf.

Equipment	Ingredients
Measuring cups and spoons Table knife Medium mixing bowl Fork Wooden spoon Cutting board Waxed paper Shallow baking pan Hot pads Small spoon	1 egg ¼ cup fine dry bread crumbs 2 tablespoons milk 1 tablespoon dried minced onion 2 teaspoons dried parsley flakes ¼ teaspoon salt ¼ teaspoon dried marjoram, crushed, *or* Italian seasoning Dash pepper 1 pound ground raw turkey 1 1½-ounce block Swiss *or* mozzarella cheese ¼ cup barbecue sauce *or* catsup

1 Turn the oven to 350°. Crack the egg into the mixing bowl. With the fork, beat the egg lightly till the yolk and white are mixed. Add the bread crumbs, milk, dried onion, dried parsley, salt, marjoram or Italian seasoning, and pepper. Stir with the fork to mix well.

2 Use your hands to break up the ground turkey as you add it to the mixture in the bowl. Mix well using your hands or a wooden spoon.

3 On the cutting board, use the table knife to cut the cheese into 4 long pieces. Place a sheet of waxed paper on the counter or table. Put the turkey mixture on the waxed paper. Divide the turkey mixture into 4 equal portions. Mold each portion around a cheese stick. Then shape each into a small loaf. Put the loaves in the baking pan.

4 Put the pan in the oven. Bake for 25 minutes. Use the hot pads to remove the pan from the oven. With the small spoon, spoon barbecue sauce or catsup over each loaf. Put the pan back in the oven. Bake about 5 minutes more or till no pink color is left in the meat. To check loaves, cut one open. Remove the pan from the oven. Turn off the oven. Serves 4.

No-Cook Chicken Salad Burritos

A flour tortilla holds a cool and creamy chicken, cucumber, and cheese filling.

Equipment	Ingredients
Measuring cups and spoons	1 5- *or* 6¾-ounce can chunk-style chicken *or* turkey
Colander	1 small cucumber
Medium mixing bowl	½ of a 4-ounce package (½ cup) shredded cheddar *or* Swiss cheese
Can opener	3 tablespoons creamy buttermilk salad dressing
Fork	4 7-inch flour tortillas
Cutting board	½ cup torn lettuce
Sharp knife	
Clear plastic wrap	

1 Put the colander over the mixing bowl. Empty the chicken or turkey into the colander so the liquid drains into the bowl. Throw away the liquid. Put the chicken or turkey into the bowl. Break up the meat using the fork.

2 On the cutting board, use the sharp knife to cut the cucumber in half. (Wrap half of the cucumber in plastic wrap and refrigerate to use another time.) Cut the end from the remaining cucumber half. Throw away the end. Cut the remaining cucumber lengthwise in half. Place the 2 pieces flat on the cutting board. Chop each piece into small pieces.

3 Add the cucumber, cheese, and salad dressing to the chicken or turkey. Stir with the fork to mix.

4 Spoon *one-fourth* of the chicken mixture near one edge of one tortilla. Top with *one-fourth* of the lettuce. Fold the edge nearest the filling over the filling just till it is covered. Then, roll up the tortilla. Repeat 3 more times to make 4 burritos. Serves 2.

Tuna Pizza Squares

Our kid-testers especially liked the crunchy topping of french-fried onions.

Equipment

Paper towel *or*
  waxed paper
13x9x2-inch baking
  pan
Colander
Medium mixing bowl
Can opener
Small spoon
Hot pads
Table knife
Pancake turner

Ingredients

Shortening
1 10-ounce package
  refrigerated pizza
  dough
1 6½- *or* 7-ounce can
  tuna
1 8-ounce package
  (2 cups) shredded
  mozzarella cheese
1 8-ounce can pizza
  sauce
1 2½-ounce jar sliced
  mushrooms
1 2.8-ounce can
  french-fried
  onions

1 Turn the oven to 425°. Put a little shortening on a piece of paper towel or waxed paper. Spread the shortening over the bottom of the baking pan to grease it.

2 Unroll the pizza dough. Press the dough into the greased pan. Press the edges against the side of the pan to make a rim.

3 Place the colander over the mixing bowl. Empty the tuna into the colander, letting the liquid run into the bowl. Throw the liquid away. Save the tuna until Step 5.

4 Sprinkle *half* of the cheese over the crust. With the back of the small spoon, spread the pizza sauce over the layer of cheese.

5 Arrange the tuna over the sauce. Drain the mushrooms in the colander the same way you drained the tuna. Arrange the mushrooms over the tuna. Sprinkle with remaining cheese.

6 Put the pan in the oven. Bake for 15 minutes. With hot pads, remove the pan from the oven. Sprinkle french-fried onions on top. Return the pan to the oven. Bake for 3 to 5 minutes more or till the crust is brown. Remove the pan from the oven. Turn off the oven.

7 With the table knife, cut the pizza into squares. With the pancake turner, lift squares from pan. Makes 4 servings.

Tadpole-in-a-Hole

Corn bread bakes around the tiny sausage "tadpoles."

Equipment

Paper towel *or*
  waxed paper
8x8x2-inch baking
  dish *or* pan
Table knife
Medium mixing bowl
Fork
Can opener
Wooden spoon
Rubber scraper
Kitchen scissors
Paper towels
Hot pads
Pancake turner

Ingredients

Shortening
1 egg
1 12-ounce can
  vacuum-packed
  whole kernel corn
1 4-ounce package
  (1 cup) shredded
  cheddar cheese
1 7- *or* 8½-ounce
  package corn
  muffin mix
1 5½-ounce package
  small smoked
  sausage links

1 Turn the oven to 400°. Put some shortening on a piece of paper towel or waxed paper. Spread the shortening over the bottom and sides of the baking dish or pan to grease it.

2 Crack the egg into the mixing bowl. With the fork, beat the egg till the yolk and the white are mixed.

3 Add *undrained* corn and *half* of the cheese to the egg. Mix well with the wooden spoon. Add the dry muffin mix. Stir till the dry ingredients are wet. (The batter will be thick.)

4 Spoon the batter into the baking dish. With the rubber scraper, scrape the batter from the bowl into the dish.

5 With the scissors, cut open the package of sausages. With paper towels, pat dry the sausage links. Arrange sausage links on top of the batter.

6 Put the dish into the oven. Bake about 30 minutes or till the top is golden. With hot pads, remove the baking dish from the oven. Turn off oven.

7 Sprinkle with the remaining cheese. Let stand 5 minutes before serving. Cut into squares. With the pancake turner, lift the squares from the baking dish. Makes 4 servings.

A Spaghetti Dinner

Give your parents a day off from kitchen chores by making this spaghetti dinner. The spaghetti and sauce cook in one pan while the bread heats in the oven.

Saucepan Spaghetti
Cheesy Garlic Bread
Lettuce with dressing
Milk

Saucepan Spaghetti

Cheesy Garlic
Bread

Dinner Countdown

Dazzle your family with your cooking skills. Just follow these easy steps.

1 Make the Cheesy Garlic Bread through Step 3.

2 Make the Saucepan Spaghetti. Set the timer for 30 minutes when told to in the recipe.

3 After the spaghetti has cooked 10 minutes, put the Cheesy Garlic Bread in the oven.

4 Rinse lettuce under cold water. Tear into bite-size pieces. Pat dry with paper towels.

5 When the timer rings, dish up the spaghetti. Take the bread from the oven. Call your family to dinner.

Robyn

Cheesy Garlic Bread

Equipment	Ingredients
Measuring spoons Small saucepan Pastry brush Table knife Heavy foil Ruler	¼ cup margarine *or* butter 1 10-inch loaf sliced French bread Garlic powder 5 1-ounce slices American *or* process Swiss cheese

1 Turn the oven to 400°. Put margarine in the saucepan. Put pan on burner. Turn burner to low. Heat till the margarine is melted. Remove from burner.

2 With the pastry brush, brush each side of the bread slices with margarine. Sprinkle lightly with garlic powder. Cut cheese slices in half diagonally.

3 Tear off a 20-inch-long piece of foil. Put the loaf back together on the foil. Place cheese slices between the bread slices. Wrap the foil around the loaf.

4 Put the loaf in oven. Bake for 20 minutes. Serves 10.

Saucepan Spaghetti

To crush oregano and basil, rub them between your fingers before adding to the sauce.

Equipment

Measuring cups
  and spoons
3-quart saucepan
  with lid
Wooden spoon
Colander
Medium mixing bowl
Large spoon
Can opener

Ingredients

1 pound ground beef
   or ground raw
   turkey
2½ cups water
1 15-ounce can
   tomato sauce
1 tablespoon dried
   minced onion
1 teaspoon dried
   oregano, crushed
½ teaspoon dried
   basil, crushed
¼ teaspoon salt
¼ teaspoon garlic
   powder
¼ teaspoon pepper
6 ounces spaghetti
   Grated Parmesan
   cheese (if you
   like)

1 Use your hands to break up the meat as you put it into the saucepan. Put the pan on the burner. Turn the burner to medium-high. Cook the meat, stirring with the wooden spoon, till no pink color is left. Turn off the burner.

2 Place the colander over the mixing bowl. Spoon the ground meat into the colander with the large spoon. Let the fat drain into the bowl. Spoon the ground meat back into the saucepan. Put the fat in a container to throw it away.

3 Stir water, tomato sauce, onion, oregano, basil, salt, garlic powder, and pepper into the pan with the meat. Put the pan on the burner. Turn the burner to high.

4 Cook till the mixture is bubbly. Break the spaghetti in half. Add the spaghetti to the saucepan. Turn the burner to low. Put the lid on the pan. Simmer about 30 minutes or till the spaghetti is tender when you bite it. Stir the spaghetti often with the wooden spoon.

5 When the spaghetti is done, turn off the burner. Remove the pan from the burner. Serve the spaghetti with Parmesan cheese, if you like. Serves 4.

Vegetable Nibbles

When a snack attack strikes, these simple vegetable fix-ups offer a tasty cure.

Spread a slice of *whole wheat bread* with *soft-style cream cheese*. Finely chop vegetables of your choice *(carrots, broccoli, radishes, cauliflower)*. Sprinkle chopped vegetables over cream cheese. Cut bread into fourths.

Thread *zucchini or cucumber slices, cherry tomatoes,* and *green pepper squares* on wooden skewers. Serve with your favorite flavor of *sour cream dip.*

Bake one 16-ounce package of *frozen fried potato nuggets* according to package directions. To eat, dip the nuggets into *barbecue sauce, sweet and sour sauce,* or *mustard sauce.*

Stir 2 to 3 tablespoons of *mixed dried fruit bits or raisins* into *half* of an 8-ounce container of *soft-style cream cheese.* Spread on *celery* or *carrot sticks.*

Chocolate Chip Oatmeal Cookies

Robby, a kid-tester, thought raisins would be good in place of the chocolate pieces.

Equipment	Ingredients
Measuring cups and spoons	½ cup margarine *or* butter (1 stick)
Large mixing bowl	1 egg
Electric mixer	1 cup all-purpose flour
Table knife	½ cup sugar
Custard cup *or* small mixing bowl	½ cup packed brown sugar
Rubber scraper	1 teaspoon vanilla
Wooden spoon	½ teaspoon baking soda
2 small spoons	1 cup quick-cooking rolled oats
2 cookie sheets	1 6-ounce package (1 cup) semisweet chocolate pieces
Hot pads	
Pancake turner	
Cooling racks	

1 Remove the margarine or butter from the refrigerator at least 30 minutes before making the cookies.

2 Turn oven to 375°. Put margarine in large bowl. Position electric mixer over bowl. Turn mixer to medium. Beat 30 seconds. Turn off mixer.

3 Crack the egg into the custard cup. Add the egg, flour, sugar, brown sugar, vanilla, and baking soda to the margarine. Beat on medium speed about 2 minutes or till well mixed. As you mix, scrape sides of bowl with rubber scraper as needed. Turn off mixer. Use the wooden spoon to stir in oats and chocolate pieces.

4 Put enough dough on a small spoon so the dough is slightly humped. Use the other spoon to push the dough from the spoon onto the cookie sheet. Repeat to fill cookie sheet. Leave about 2 inches between cookies.

5 Put the cookie sheet in the oven. Bake 8 to 10 minutes or till brown. While the cookies bake, drop more cookie dough onto the other cookie sheet.

6 Use hot pads to remove the cookie sheet from the oven. Put the second cookie sheet into the oven. Use the pancake turner to lift the baked cookies onto the cooling rack. When the first cookie sheet is cool, drop more dough onto it. Repeat with remaining dough. Turn off the oven. Makes about 40.

Peanut Butter Honey Cookies

The dough is so soft you can mix it with a wooden spoon instead of a mixer.

Equipment	Ingredients
Measuring cups and spoons	Shortening
Paper towel	½ cup sugar
2 cookie sheets	½ cup shortening
Large mixing bowl	½ cup peanut butter
Wooden spoon	½ cup honey
Table knife	1 egg
Small mixing bowl	1½ cups all-purpose flour
Medium mixing bowl	¼ teaspoon baking soda
2 small spoons	¼ teaspoon baking powder
Hot pads	¼ teaspoon salt
Pancake turner	
Cooling racks	

1 Turn the oven to 350°. Put some shortening on a piece of paper towel. Spread the shortening over the cookie sheets to grease them.

2 In the large bowl, put the sugar, ½ cup shortening, peanut butter, and honey. Mix well with the wooden spoon.

3 Crack egg into small bowl. Add egg to the peanut butter mixture. Stir till well mixed.

4 In the medium bowl, put flour, baking soda, baking powder, and salt. Stir to mix.

5 Add the flour mixture, a spoonful at a time, to the peanut butter mixture, stirring well after each spoonful.

6 Put enough cookie dough on a small spoon so the dough is slightly humped. Use the other small spoon to push the dough from the spoon onto the cookie sheet. Repeat to fill the cookie sheet. Leave about 2 inches between cookies.

7 Put cookie sheet in the oven. Bake for 12 to 13 minutes or till edges are brown. While cookies bake, drop more dough onto the other cookie sheet.

8 With hot pads, remove the cookie sheet from the oven. Put the second cookie sheet in oven. With the pancake turner, lift baked cookies onto cooling rack. Let the first cookie sheet cool. Repeat with the remaining dough. Turn off oven. Makes 32.

Chocolate Cherry Trifle

Shannon, one of our kid-testers, rated this pudding and cake dessert as "the best."

Equipment	Ingredients
Measuring cups	½ of a 10¾-ounce frozen loaf pound cake *or* one 3-ounce package (12) ladyfingers
Wide-mouthed jar with a screw-top lid (like a mayonnaise or peanut butter jar)	1½ cups milk
Small spoon	1 4-serving-size package *instant* chocolate pudding mix
6 dessert dishes	½ of a 21-ounce can cherry pie filling
Rubber scraper	Pressurized whipped dessert topping (if you like)
Table knife	
Can opener	

1 If you use pound cake, remove the cake from the freezer. Let it stand at room temperature for 1 hour.

2 Put the milk in the jar. Add the dry pudding mix. Tightly screw the lid on the jar. Shake the jar vigorously about 1 minute or till pudding is mixed.

3 Use the small spoon to place some of the pudding into each of the dessert dishes. With the rubber scraper, scrape all the pudding from the jar.

4 Use the table knife to cut the pound cake in half. (Save half of the cake for another use.) Cut the pound cake into 6 slices. Place one slice in each dish. (If you use ladyfingers, separate each one in half. Arrange 4 ladyfinger halves in each dish.) Spoon some cherry pie filling on top of the pound cake in each dish. Top each with dessert topping, if you like. Serves 6.

Cocoa Snowballs

You can serve these snowballs in ice cream cones instead of dishes.

Equipment

Measuring cups
Medium mixing bowl
Wooden spoon
Ice cream scoop
  or large spoon
Baking sheet
4 dessert dishes

Ingredients

½ cup chocolate-
  flavored crisp
  rice cereal
¼ cup coconut
¼ cup chopped nut
  topping
1 pint ice cream
  (any flavor)

1 In the medium mixing bowl, put the cereal, coconut, and nut topping. Stir with the wooden spoon to mix.

2 Use the ice cream scoop or large spoon to scoop 4 balls of ice cream. Drop each ball, one at a time, into the cereal mixture. Roll the ball around till it is coated. Work quickly so the ice cream doesn't melt. Place the ice cream balls on the baking sheet. Put them in the freezer till serving time.

3 To serve, put an ice cream ball in each dessert dish. Makes 4 servings.

Sunshine Cupcakes

Lemon yogurt lends a sunny yellow color to these cupcakes.

Equipment	Ingredients
12 paper bake cups Muffin pan(s) for 12 cupcakes Table knife Medium mixing bowl Wooden spoon Large spoon Wooden toothpick Hot pads Cooling racks Narrow metal spatula *or* table knife	1 egg 1 package 1-layer-size yellow cake mix 1 8-ounce carton lemon, orange, pineapple, *or* vanilla yogurt ½ of a can lemon *or* vanilla frosting

1 Turn the oven to 350°. Put a paper bake cup into each muffin pan cup.

2 Crack the egg into the mixing bowl. Add the cake mix and yogurt. Use the wooden spoon to stir the batter till it is almost smooth. (The batter should be thick.)

3 Use the large spoon to fill each muffin cup ⅔ full with the batter.

4 Put the muffin pan(s) in the oven. Bake about 20 minutes or till the toothpick comes out clean when inserted near the center of a cupcake. Use the hot pads to remove the muffin pan(s) from the oven. Turn off the oven. Place the muffin pan(s) on the cooling racks. Let them cool for 10 minutes. Remove the cupcakes from the pan(s). Cool the cupcakes completely on the cooling racks.

5 Use the narrow metal spatula or table knife to frost the cupcakes with lemon or vanilla frosting. Makes 12.

Brownies

Extra chocolate and nuts top off these brownie squares.

Equipment	Ingredients
Measuring cups and spoons	Shortening
Paper towel *or* waxed paper	¼ cup margarine *or* butter
9x9x2-inch baking pan	1 5.5-ounce can chocolate-flavored syrup
Medium saucepan	½ cup all-purpose flour
Wooden spoon	⅓ cup sugar
Table knife	¼ teaspoon baking soda
Custard cup *or* small bowl	2 eggs
Fork	⅓ cup miniature semisweet chocolate pieces
Rubber scraper	⅓ cup broken walnuts *or* pecans
Wooden toothpick	
Hot pads	
Cooling rack	

1 Turn oven to 350°. Put some shortening on a piece of paper towel or waxed paper. Spread the shortening over the bottom and sides of the baking pan to grease it.

2 In the saucepan, put the margarine or butter. Put the saucepan on a burner. Turn the burner to medium-low. Heat till the margarine or butter is melted. Turn off the burner. Remove the saucepan from the burner. Use the wooden spoon to stir in chocolate syrup, flour, sugar, and baking soda.

3 Crack one of the eggs into the custard cup or small bowl. Stir with the fork till the yolk and the white are mixed. Add egg to the mixture in the saucepan. Stir till well mixed. Repeat with the remaining egg. Mix well. Pour the batter into the greased baking pan. Use the rubber scraper to scrape all the batter from the saucepan into the baking pan.

4 Put the baking pan in the oven. Bake for 18 to 20 minutes or till the toothpick comes out clean when inserted near the center. Use hot pads to remove the pan from the oven. Turn off the oven. Place the pan on the cooling rack. Sprinkle with miniature chocolate pieces and nuts. Cool. Cut brownies into squares. Makes 16.

Choice Chocolate Cake

Whenever a family birthday comes around, bake this moist, delicious cake.

Equipment

Measuring cups
  and spoons
Paper towel *or*
  waxed paper
9x1½-inch round
  baking pan
Large mixing bowl
Wooden spoon
Small saucepan
Table knife
Custard cup *or* small
  bowl
Rubber scraper
Wooden toothpick
Hot pads
2 cooling racks

Ingredients

Shortening
1 cup all-purpose
  flour
1 cup sugar
½ teaspoon baking
  soda
½ cup margarine
  or butter
½ cup water
3 tablespoons
  unsweetened
  cocoa powder
1 egg
¼ cup buttermilk
½ teaspoon vanilla
Chocolate Frosting
  (see recipe, *page
  73*) *or* 1 can
  chocolate frosting
Candy-coated milk
  chocolate pieces
  (if you like)

1 Turn the oven to 350°. Put some shortening on a piece of paper towel or waxed paper. Spread the shortening over the bottom and sides of the baking pan to grease it.

2 In the mixing bowl, put flour, sugar, and baking soda. Mix well with the wooden spoon. Save until Step 4.

3 In saucepan, put margarine, water, and cocoa powder. Put pan on burner. Turn to medium. Heat till margarine melts. Turn off burner. Remove pan from burner.

4 Crack the egg into the custard cup. Add the egg, margarine mixture, buttermilk, and vanilla to dry ingredients. Beat till smooth with the wooden spoon. Pour the batter into the greased pan. With the rubber scraper, scrape all batter from the bowl into the pan.

5 Put the pan in the oven. Bake for 25 to 30 minutes or till the toothpick comes out clean when inserted near the center. Use hot pads to remove cake from oven. Turn off oven. Cool on a cooling rack for 10 minutes. Turn cake in pan upside-down on rack. Carefully lift pan from cake. Place the second cooling rack over cake. Turn over so the rounded side of the cake is on top. Remove top cooling rack. Cool completely.

6 Frost cake with Chocolate Frosting and, if you like, decorate with candy. Serves 8.

Chocolate Frosting

A smooth and creamy frosting with a mild chocolate flavor.

Equipment

Measuring cups
and spoons
Strainer
Waxed paper
Large spoon
Small saucepan
Medium mixing bowl
Wooden spoon

Ingredients

Powdered sugar
(about 1½ cups)
3 tablespoons
margarine *or*
butter
2 tablespoons
unsweetened
cocoa powder
1 tablespoon milk
½ teaspoon vanilla

1 To sift the powdered sugar, place the strainer over a sheet of waxed paper. Put the powdered sugar in the strainer. Use the large spoon to stir the sugar so it falls through the strainer. Measure 1½ cups of sifted sugar. Save until Step 3.

2 Put margarine in the saucepan. Put the saucepan on burner. Turn burner to low. Heat till margarine melts. Turn off burner. Remove pan. Pour melted margarine into the bowl.

3 Add the cocoa powder. Stir with the wooden spoon till well mixed. Add about *half* of the powdered sugar, and all the milk and vanilla. Stir gently till mixed (mixture will be lumpy). Then, beat with wooden spoon till mixture is smooth.

4 Slowly add the rest of the powdered sugar, beating well. Beat in more milk, if needed, to make the frosting soft enough to spread. Use it to frost Choice Chocolate Cake. Makes about 1 cup.

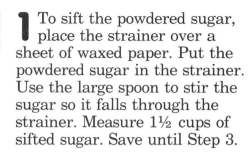 **Microwave Directions**

Follow Step 1 as directed above. Put the margarine or butter in a *microwave-safe medium mixing bowl.* Set oven on high power. Micro-cook about 1 minute or till margarine melts. Follow Steps 3 and 4 as directed above.

Nut-Cracker Sweets

Leave a few of these brown-sugar-topped graham crackers for Santa on Christmas Eve.

Equipment

Measuring cups
Ruler
Foil
15x10x1-inch baking
  pan
Small saucepan
Wooden spoon
Hot pads
Cooling rack

Ingredients

⅓ cup margarine
  or butter
⅓ cup packed brown
  sugar
12 graham crackers
⅔ cup chopped nut
  topping

1 Turn the oven to 350°. Tear off a 15-inch piece of foil. Line the baking pan with the foil. Save until Step 3.

2 Put the margarine or butter in the saucepan. Put the pan on the burner. Turn the burner to low. Heat till the margarine melts. Turn off the burner. Remove the saucepan from the burner. With the wooden spoon, stir in brown sugar. Mix well. Save until Step 4.

3 Arrange graham crackers, side by side, in the foil-lined baking pan.

4 Stir the brown sugar mixture. Spoon the brown sugar mixture over the graham crackers. Sprinkle the crackers with the nut topping.

5 Put the pan in the oven. Bake for 7 to 9 minutes or till the topping is bubbly. Use hot pads to remove the pan from the oven. Turn off the oven. Put the pan on the cooling rack. When crackers are cool, break each cracker into four pieces along the lines in the crackers. Store crackers in a tightly covered container. Makes 48.

Ice Cream-Cookie Sundaes

Chad, one of our kid-testers, called this dessert a banana split with a hidden cookie.

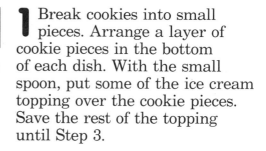

Equipment	Ingredients

Measuring cups
4 dessert dishes
Small spoon
Table knife
Ice cream scoop
  or large spoon
	4 soft oatmeal cookies
	  (2 to 3 inches in
	  diameter)
	¼ cup butterscotch,
	  chocolate, *or*
	  caramel ice cream
	  topping
	1 small banana
	2 cups vanilla *or*
	  chocolate ice
	  cream
	¼ cup peanuts

1 Break cookies into small pieces. Arrange a layer of cookie pieces in the bottom of each dish. With the small spoon, put some of the ice cream topping over the cookie pieces. Save the rest of the topping until Step 3.

2 Peel the banana. Slice it with the table knife. Arrange some banana slices in each dish.

3 Use the ice cream scoop or large spoon to place ice cream into each dessert dish. Spoon the remaining ice cream topping over the ice cream. Sprinkle each serving with some peanuts.

4 Top each dessert with pressurized whipped dessert topping, if you like. Serve right away. Makes 4 servings.

Basic Food Groups

To feel your best, look your best, and perform your best, you need to eat a variety of foods. And, that's easy to do. Simply choose several servings a day from each of the Basic Food Groups. The meal below shows a typical food from each of the groups.

Fruits-Vegetables
The fruit-and-vegetable group supplies our bodies with fiber and vitamins A and C. You need four or more servings from this group every day.

Milk
The milk group includes milk, cheese, yogurt, pudding, ice milk, and ice cream. These foods supply our bodies with calcium, riboflavin, and protein. You need at least three servings from this group every day.

Other Foods

This group includes foods that don't fit the other categories. Such items as soda pop, jelly, candies, desserts, margarine, and butter make up this food group. Since these foods contain mostly sugar and fat, don't eat too many of them.

Meat

The meat group includes beef, veal, pork, lamb, poultry, fish, eggs, nuts, and dried beans. These provide us with protein, iron, niacin, and thiamine. You should eat two servings from this group each day.

Breads-Cereals

The bread-and-cereal group includes breads, cereals, rice, and pasta. This group fuels our bodies with carbohydrates, thiamine, iron, niacin, and fiber. You need four or more servings from this group each day.

Nutrition Analysis

Per Serving

Recipes	Servings	Calories	Protein (grams)	Carbohydrates (grams)	Fat (grams)	Sodium (milligrams)	Potassium (milligrams)	Cholesterol (milligrams)
All-American Hamburgers (p. 43)	4	352	23	21	19	284	259	79
Applesauce Breakfast Cake (p. 14)	9	215	3	27	11	105	68	31
Apple Snapple Oatmeal (p. 19)	4	248	5	54	2	8	429	0
Baked Ham Omelet (p. 11)	6	276	18	2	21	509	221	578
Banana-Berry Drink (p. 25)	2	178	7	32	3	97	544	12
Banana Shakes (p. 26)	2	372	9	50	16	163	637	67
Beef 'n' Slaw Pockets (p. 41)	4	299	18	21	16	837	176	62
Brownies (p. 71)	16	126	2	16	7	65	65	34
Cheeseburgers (p. 43)	4	405	26	21	23	484	282	92
Cheesy Garlic Bread (p. 62)	10	196	6	20	10	460	57	14
Chicken and Biscuit Dinners (p. 54)	4	274	19	21	13	866	303	48
Chicken Chow Mein (p. 48)	4	250	20	23	9	660	378	49
Chicken Club Croissants (p. 46)	4	369	20	21	22	294	190	51
Chicken Pocket Burgers (p. 37)	4	395	16	30	24	548	242	73
Chili-on-Muffins (p. 50)	4	541	30	45	28	1,485	731	121
Chocolate Cherry Trifle (p. 68)	6	341	4	69	6	195	128	52
Chocolate Chip Oatmeal Cookies (p. 66)	40	83	1	11	4	43	36	7
Chocolate French Toast (p. 12)	2	366	13	34	19	508	231	281
Chocolate Frosting (p. 73)	8	115	0	19	5	61	14	0
Choice Chocolate Cake (p. 72)	8	393	3	58	18	295	69	35
Cocoa-on-Call (p. 32)	10	143	10	26	1	174	471	5
Cocoa Snowballs (p. 69)	4	219	4	23	13	87	188	30
Cool and Creamy Fruit Cup (p. 18)	4	125	3	28	1	35	344	2
Dip-It Sauce with Vegetables (p. 47)	4	155	9	3	12	300	87	8
First-Place Crispy Chicken (p. 49)	4	318	36	13	13	278	407	170
Fruit Lover's Pops (p. 28)	10	67	1	16	0	32	113	0
Grilled Cheese and More (p. 40)	1	502	23	29	32	1,559	236	70
Honey Limeade (p. 27)	6	114	0	30	0	7	35	0
Hot Dog! It's Macaroni! (p. 55)	4	509	27	31	30	1,681	356	115
Hot Tuna Buns (p. 39)	3	419	26	21	26	754	272	78
Ice Cream-Cookie Sundaes (p. 75)	4	341	7	48	15	102	393	38
Jack-O'-Lantern Loaf (p. 30)	18	149	2	24	5	92	97	31

Recipes	Servings	Calories	Protein (grams)	Carbohydrates (grams)	Fat (grams)	Sodium (milligrams)	Potassium (milligrams)	Cholesterol (milligrams)
Just-My-Size Pizzas (p. 23)	12	130	6	13	6	391	47	9
Malted Milk Shakes (p. 26)	2	403	11	52	18	259	559	71
Milk Chocolate Bubble Ring (p. 33)	10	309	4	40	15	651	81	2
Milk Shakes (p. 26)	2	317	8	36	16	163	400	67
Nachos (p. 22)	4	93	3	9	5	152	23	6
No-Cook Chicken Salad Burritos (p. 57)	2	469	26	32	28	817	278	74
Nut-Cracker Sweets (p. 74)	48	36	0	4	2	39	24	0
Oatmeal Cinnamon Muffins (p. 15)	12	161	3	24	6	111	131	24
Peanut Butter Honey Cookies (p. 67)	32	104	2	12	6	49	38	9
Peanut Butter Shakes (p. 26)	2	411	12	39	24	238	509	67
Peanut Butter Surprise Balls (p. 24)	25	46	2	3	3	38	69	1
Pint-Sized Heros (p. 38)	4	327	23	24	15	953	265	59
Pop-and-Crunch Snack Mix (p. 31)	16	137	4	14	8	122	85	0
Raisin Pancake Squares (p. 13)	6	293	7	47	9	688	271	50
Reuben-Style Pockets (p. 41)	4	319	18	20	18	890	158	63
Saucepan Spaghetti (p. 63)	4	429	27	41	17	826	740	77
Scrambled Eggs (p. 10)	4	191	13	2	14	312	156	551
Seafood Salad (p. 52)	4	230	12	24	9	787	418	20
Shake-a-Snack (p. 27)	24	94	2	12	4	2	86	0
Sloppy Toms (p. 36)	8	262	20	24	9	510	307	50
Strawberry Pink Shakes (p. 29)	3	312	6	50	11	121	390	46
Sunshine Cupcakes (p. 70)	12	199	2	33	6	140	65	24
Super Supper Salad (p. 53)	4	253	19	4	18	1,003	343	62
Taco Cheeseburgers (p. 42)	8	169	11	8	10	191	168	38
Taco Flats (p. 51)	4	407	21	29	23	1,136	619	63
Tadpole-in-a-Hole (p. 59)	4	568	22	53	30	1,336	371	125
Tuna Pizza Squares (p. 58)	4	566	37	47	25	1,145	299	60
Tuna Salad Sandwiches (p. 39)	3	347	23	28	17	467	355	51
Turkey Mini Loaves (p. 56)	4	250	31	9	9	412	352	144

This information helps you keep tabs on what you eat. We analyzed recipes using the first choice when ingredient options are given and using the first serving size if a serving range is given. We also omitted optional ingredients.

Index

A-B

All-American Hamburgers, 43
Applesauce Breakfast Cake, 14
Apple Snapple Oatmeal, 19
Backyard Lunch, 44
Baked Ham Omelet, 11
Banana-Berry Drink, 25
Banana Shakes, 26
Beef
  All-American
    Hamburgers, 43
  Beef 'n' Slaw Pockets, 41
  Cheeseburgers, 43
  Chili-on-Muffins, 50
  Pint-Sized Heros, 38
  Reuben-Style Pockets, 41
  Saucepan Spaghetti, 63
  Sloppy Toms, 36
  Taco Cheeseburgers, 42
  Taco Flats, 51
Bread Spreads, 20
Brownies, 71

C

Cheeseburgers, 43
Cheesy Garlic Bread, 62
Chicken
  Chicken and Biscuit
    Dinners, 54
  Chicken Chow Mein, 48
  Chicken Club Croissants, 46
  Chicken Pocket Burgers, 37
  First-Place Crispy
    Chicken, 49
  Grilled Cheese and More, 40
  No-Cook Chicken Salad
    Burritos, 57
  Super Supper Salad, 53
Chili-on-Muffins, 50
Chocolate
  Brownies, 71
  Chocolate Cherry Trifle, 68
  Chocolate Chip Oatmeal
    Cookies, 66
  Chocolate French Toast, 12
  Chocolate Frosting, 73
  Choice Chocolate Cake, 72
  Cocoa-on-Call, 32
  Cocoa Snowballs, 69
  Milk Chocolate Bubble
    Ring, 31

Choice Chocolate Cake, 72
Cocoa-on-Call, 32
Cocoa Snowballs, 69
Cookies
  Chocolate Chip Oatmeal
    Cookies, 66
  Peanut Butter Honey
    Cookies, 67
Cool and Creamy Fruit
  Cup, 18

D-L

Dip-It Sauce with
  Vegetables, 47
Drinks
  Banana-Berry Drink, 25
  Banana Shakes, 26
  Cocoa-on-Call, 32
  Honey Limeade, 27
  Malted Milk Shakes, 26
  Milk Shakes, 26
  Peanut Butter Shakes, 26
  Strawberry Pink Shakes, 29
Early Bird's Breakfast, 16
First-Place Crispy Chicken, 49
Fruit Fix-Ups, 34
Fruit Lover's Pops, 28
Grilled Cheese and More, 40
Ham
  Grilled Cheese and More, 40
  Pint-Sized Heros, 38
  Super Supper Salad, 53
  Taco Cheeseburgers, 42
Honey Limeade, 27
Hot Dog! It's Macaroni!, 55
Hot Tuna Buns, 39
Ice Cream-Cookie Sundaes, 75
Jack-O'-Lantern Loaf, 30
Just-My-Size Pizzas, 23

M-S

Malted Milk Shakes, 26
Milk Chocolate Bubble
  Ring, 33
Milk Shakes, 26
Nachos, 22
No-Cook Chicken Salad
  Burritos, 57
Nut-Cracker Sweets, 74
Oatmeal Cinnamon
  Muffins, 15

Peanut Butter Honey
  Cookies, 67
Peanut Butter Shakes, 26
Peanut Butter Surprise
  Balls, 24
Pint-Sized Heros, 38
Pop-and-Crunch Snack Mix, 31
Raisin Pancake Squares, 13
Reuben-Style Pockets, 41
Saucepan Spaghetti, 63
Scrambled Eggs, 10
Seafood Salad, 52
Shake-a-Snack, 27
Sloppy Toms, 36
Strawberry Pink Shakes, 29
Spaghetti Dinner, 60
Sunshine Cupcakes, 70
Super Supper Salad, 53

T-Z

Taco Cheeseburgers, 42
Taco Flats, 51
Tadpole-in-a-Hole, 59
Tuna
  Hot Tuna Buns, 39
  Tuna Pizza Squares, 58
  Tuna Salad Sandwiches, 39
Turkey
  Chicken and Biscuit
    Dinners, 54
  Chicken Club Croissants, 46
  Grilled Cheese and More, 40
  No-Cook Chicken Salad
    Burritos, 57
  Pint-Sized Heros, 38
  Saucepan Spaghetti, 63
  Sloppy Toms, 36
  Supper Super Salad, 53
  Turkey Mini Loaves, 56
Vegetable Nibbles, 64